PEOPLE MATTER®

# PEOPLE MATTER®

## Driving **Productivity**, **Efficiency** and **Profits** through Happier Team Members

## NATE DAPORE

President and CEO of PeopleMatter

Published by Advantage, Charleston, South Carolina.
Member of Advantage Media Group.

ADVANTAGE is a registered trademark and the Advantage colophon is a trademark of Advantage Media Group, Inc.

Printed in the United States of America.

ISBN: 978-1-59932-457-9
LCCN: 2014938311

This publication is designed to provide accurate and authoritative information in regard to the subject matter covered. It is sold with the understanding that the publisher is not engaged in rendering legal, accounting, or other professional services. If legal advice or other expert assistance is required, the services of a competent professional person should be sought.

Book design by Amy Ropp.

Advantage Media Group is proud to be a part of the Tree Neutral® program. Tree Neutral offsets the number of trees consumed in the production and printing of this book by taking proactive steps such as planting trees in direct proportion to the number of trees used to print books. To learn more about Tree Neutral, please visit www.treeneutral.com. To learn more about Advantage's commitment to being a responsible steward of the environment, please visit www.advantagefamily.com/green

Advantage Media Group is a publisher of business, self-improvement, and professional development books and online learning. We help entrepreneurs, business leaders, and professionals share their Stories, Passion, and Knowledge to help others Learn & Grow. Do you have a manuscript or book idea that you would like us to consider for publishing? Please visit advantagefamily.com or call 1.866.775.1696.

# Contents

# Foreword

By **Louis Basile**, Founder and CEO of Wildflower Bread Company

**WHEN I DECIDED TO START** the Wildflower Bread Company, what I really wanted to do was to create a WOW dining experience for everyone to enjoy, provide a work environment that was built on mutual respect for all and to make a difference in the communities in which we operate restaurants. To this day these continue to be the driving forces behind the Wildflower Bread Company.

We wanted to give people the opportunity to gather in a comfortable, clean place that they called their own, where the food is outstanding and the service is great. When people get together in a place like this, lots of interesting conversations happen, memories are created, and traditions are formed. This type of environment creates favorite moments, funny moments, sad moments and compelling moments for everyone.

Of course, the key to all this is having an incredible group of people committed to delivering such an experience. Our team members—better known as "Breadheads"—are the reason for our success and the reason why people love coming to Wildflower again and again. Our Breadheads are passionate about serving great food and preserving the art of making world class artisan bread. It is driving forces like this that get our Breadheads really excited about delivering an incredible experience to our guests. Without committed Breadheads, we would have never grown from one restaurant in November 1996 to the 14 we now operate in Arizona.

We started our first restaurant with the typical independent restaurant marketing plan, which is word of mouth, and, while we were passionate and enthusiastic about the Wildflower brand, we had minimal expectations about who and how many customers would show up for our first day of business in November of 1996. Much to my surprise, lots of people showed up; starting on the very first day and to this day, we are incredibly grateful that Wildflower Fans continue to choose the Wildflower. Of course, when you deliver an experience that is truly compelling to consumers, they will come back time and time again. That's what we've done for the past 17 years, and it's how we've continued to grow our business.

We're a purpose- and values-driven company, and I've always believed that Wildflower is about much more than just serving food or making money. We are about building relationships and connecting with people; we're about giving back to the communities we call home. We wanted to define our purpose in a way that the entire Wildflower team could stand behind, rally around and live by. I had a feeling that our purpose was something that was bigger than all of us. Ultimately, it was a team of Breadheads who decided why we exist. They were dubbed the Slice Team because these Breadheads were a cross-section of everyone who worked at the Wildflower. It is the Slice Team that came up with our purpose statement: "We change lives, create traditions, build community and feed the soul with passion. Every time, every day!"

I remember as if it was yesterday, being so proud and somewhat scared, when we settled on the Wildflower purpose. The fact of the matter is that the Slice Team went deeper and dreamed bigger then I had ever imagined. As their leader, I was both in awe of what they had created as our purpose/true north and I questioned my own ability to honor and be the role model for what they believed was the

Wildflower purpose. It truly is amazing what a group of people can accomplish working together as a team with a common vision and goal. Our purpose, along with our values—which were also created by the same Slice Team of Breadheads—have been and continue to be, incredibly impactful for our brand. These two pieces guide everything we do at Wildflower, for everyone from our line cooks to our executive team. I think it's especially important for Breadheads to see our leadership team living our values and purpose, rather than talking about them. Our daily intention is to honor our purpose and use our values, all the time, in order to ensure that we deliver an outstanding experience to our Breadheads, customers and community. Our culture helps people feel that the company they work for is a great place to work.

Because the workforce tends to be transient and turnover is high in the restaurant industry, some companies do not believe it's worth the effort to invest in people, because those people are not going to be around long enough to see the fruits of their efforts. From my perspective, I feel *we have to invest in people*; we have a responsibility to give more than we ask to everybody who comes into contact with the Wildflower. Or, if you want to look at it from a purely business perspective, if you don't treat your team members well, then how can you expect them to treat your customers well? I have this dream and I work tirelessly to see it through, that every Breadhead who has ever worked here will say that this is the best place they have ever worked.

I believe that the restaurant business has always been about one customer at a time, and I want our Breadheads to understand and believe that they are making a difference each and every day. In this business, we are rewarded for our operational discipline and execution. When someone has a favorite dish, they want it to taste the same every time they dine with us. The repetitiveness of these daily tasks can become incredibly mundane, and sometime the daily tasks can become so monotonous that the team members become disinterested. In my opinion, if you don't provide your team members with a higher reason for getting out of bed in the morning and coming to work, then you'll end up with incredibly mediocre results. If your team members think that their only purpose is to flip a burger or make a sandwich the way the company wants it to be made, then I know you won't achieve the level of engagement that you want and need with today's workforce to be successful. Everyone wants to be appreciated. *All of us want to believe that what we do matters.*

One of the things I like to do to help our Breadheads understand that what they do matters is to ask them how they have changed somebody's life today. I get all sorts of answers, from simply, "by making someone smile" or, "by going the extra mile to open the door for someone," to some really interesting ones that make me sit and think, "wow, that's incredible."

For example, we have a regular customer at one of our restaurants whose husband recently passed away. She and her husband had been coming to eat at the restaurant every morning for 17 years. Well, this new widow still came to our restaurant every day after her husband passed, and the Breadheads who worked there could tell that she was really sad. So they all rallied around her to let her know that we care for her like family. They asked her how she was doing every morning and gave her some extra attention. She's been incredibly grateful for that network of Breadheads and customers who sincerely care about her and who have made her part of their Wildflower family.

I, too, like to look for ways that I can change people's lives every day. Not long ago, one of our customers tweeted that she didn't feel well and that all she wanted was some Wildflower soup. I happened to be on Twitter at the time, so I tweeted back, "Maybe we can deliver some soup to you." We don't deliver but we worked it out and ended up bringing her the soup she so needed. It was just a small token of our appreciation for her as a Wildflower Fan and as a person. This is also an example of the pay-it-forward model that I live by: if you do good deeds, good things will happen to you. I model this for our Breadheads, and we all try to live by the pay-it-forward model to make a daily difference.

I don't believe a silver bullet for what makes a business successful exists. I do believe that success can be found in the simple idea that you have to be respectful of people and that when you provide people with a purpose—something that is compelling and resonates with them—a shift in their performance occurs, which helps ensure the future success of the brand.  In my opinion, companies that figure this out are the ones that are the most successful today. And the companies that don't, will be the ones that continue to struggle.

Our purpose and our values are not just internally applied. What I like about being the founder and owner of a small business is that I get to choose who we do business with. I believe everything in life is about choices, and it's great to be able to do business with folks who are like-minded in terms of how they think about their business, how they treat their people, and their level of community involvement. The reality is that it's always more fun when you're partnering with people you not only like, but who also share a similar position on social and business issues. That's a big reason why we do business with PeopleMatter. They are at the crossroads of where technology and business management come together. They have helped us manage all the nuances of the human resources side of the business. Simply put, they are a company that believes people truly matter.

**—LOUIS BASILE,**
Founder and CEO of Wildflower Bread Company

# Introduction

**I WAS MOTIVATED TO WRITE THIS BOOK** based on the experiences I have had over the past five years while working with the service industry, by which I mean restaurants, hotels, convenience stores, and retail businesses, and the wonderful people I have come into contact with—the owners, the operators, the team members, and the store associates. There are a ton of books out there on culture and there are a ton of books on how to improve your business, but I don't feel like there is a book that really speaks to the audience that we serve every day. I have seen the changes that a software company can make in these businesses—to both their bottom lines and their company cultures—and I have seen how we can help make these workplaces better, with the end result being happier employees, which in turn leads to happier customers. I have seen how businesses can really drive productivity, efficiency and profits by making sure their people matter.

........................................

I grew up in Charleston, South Carolina. I was actually was born in Lima, Ohio, but my parents moved to Charleston in 1979. I was raised in the South, and back then it was a very blue-blood society, so I was kind of an outsider from my early days in Charleston. My first job was at Swensen's Ice Cream store down at the City Market in Charleston, where I scooped ice cream during the summer at the ripe old age of 15.

That was my first real exposure to the restaurant industry and to the customer service aspect of a job. It was a job that could be more than a little monotonous at times. You are scooping ice cream and you are asking people over and over and over again what flavor they want. Do they want a cup or a cone? Do they want one scoop or two? You ask those three questions again and again over a six- to eight-hour shift. You have to always put a smile on when you ask. You have to always be a happy, pleasant person to talk to. You have to help make someone's experience with ice cream memorable. Whether I was serving a couple on a date, a child getting her first taste of ice cream, or someone coming in for a birthday treat, I always tried to keep that smile and positive attitude.

Despite the monotony, it was a great place to work. The team was excited to be there, and I think that made a big difference. I still remember the manager, who was a fun person to work for and someone who really cared about people.

I went to Bishop England High School, a Catholic high school in Charleston, and then on to Hampden-Sydney College in Virginia. That's when I first started to get excited about technology. There were two what I would call "defining moments" in my life during that time, which led me in the technology direction. One was the first time I ever went on the Internet, which was back in the spring of 1995, when I was in my junior year of high school. I still remember it as if it were yesterday. I had used the old dial-up America Online before, but the Netscape browser I used that day showed me what the Internet truly was. It was during a visit to Hampden-Sydney, where I went to see some older friends. They had Internet access in their dorm rooms, and I remember going on that Netscape browser and being captivated by it. I'm not even sure why. I think I just sensed that this was a tremendous opportunity to change communication, to really change the way people interact with one another. And to have all this information at your fingertips—there was so much power in that. I didn't know how it was all going to play out, but I sensed that a huge change was going to happen.

The second big catalyst was a talk given by Greyson Quarles, the CFO of SAS Institute and an alumnus of Hampden-Sydney. He was speaking to an economics class about the company he worked for—which, at the time, was the largest privately held software company in the world—and the global changes they were making. SAS connected technology and data in a way that revolutionized the agricultural industry. Its software was able to predict and even increase crop yields, leading to a huge impact on our global economy. That example showed me how technology could really change people's lives.

I went to work for SAS right out of college for a short time. When I was looking to leave, I called a friend who was running a group called ThinkTEC, which was part of the Charleston Metro Chamber of Commerce and was trying to lure technology companies to the Charleston area. I half-jokingly asked him, "Are there any tech start-ups in Charleston?" He said, "There are a couple of guys in Mount Pleasant who are trying to start a benefits enrollment software company. I don't know if you would really be interested in that, but you may want to take a look."

I asked if he could introduce me to the CEO, Shawn Jenkins, and he did. That was in the fall of 2000, and Shawn and I met for a burrito at La Hacienda, a Mexican restaurant, which is still there on Highway 17 North in Mount Pleasant. You can see restaurants have played a big role in my life.

Shawn and I connected over the fact that we were both passionate sales guys, had both sold cars during our careers, and had been through the ups and downs that come with the sales territory. I had worked at Stokes Mazda Volkswagen in North Charleston and learned a lot about customer service on that job. There were a bunch of salespeople there who would look at someone who came on the lot and stereotype him or her right away as "somebody who couldn't buy anything so why waste your time." But not me. I would always spend the same amount of time and put the same amount of high-level energy into serving all customers, regardless of their appearance or what they drove up in. It paid off too. One couple, for example, looked a bit rough, so I was the only one who would talk to them. They ended up buying a $60,000 Mazda Millennium and had perfect credit. I just had an instinct that looks could be deceiving and believed that you had to treat every customer with respect and dignity, no matter what. That view led me to become the salesman of the month in my very first month on the job. I was only 19 years old.

Shawn and I started talking about the car business, and we just hit it off. He asked me if I would work for him, and that's how I became one of the first sales guys at Benefitfocus. I started there in January 2001 and worked with that company for eight years. Those were eight great years of helping build a start-up software-as-a-service company into a billion-dollar business and the nation's largest provider of benefits software. I really honed my passion for technology and for human resources software during that time. It was a dream come true for me. I was working with people and technology, and I was part of a company that was growing rapidly. It was also a company that really impacted people's lives. Insurance benefits may sound like boring stuff to some, but they are really important to people. That becomes obvious the first time you help people get their newborn child onto their health plan or pick out a benefits package for their family.

The first customer I had at Benefitfocus was a guy named Roger Foreman from Blue Cross Blue Shield of Kansas City. He was willing to take a risk with me and with the company when it was still very much just a start-up, which led to us to develop a lifelong friendship. Both of us have left our respective companies, but we are still good friends today and get together every year for a Cubs game in the summer. I believe that *the customer relationship should transcend a mere business transaction,* and our friendship is testament to that. Your customers have to be people you genuinely care about. You have to have their best interests at heart. In the end, I believe Roger wanted to do business with us because he really enjoyed working with me and saw in me somebody who was committed to his success. I put his wants and needs ahead of my own. I always worked hard to make sure that the client was well served and taken care of.

Another example of the true passion for the customer that we had at Benefitfocus was when a bunch of us had a big sales call at Blue Cross Blue Shield of Massachusetts. One of the great things I learned at Benefitfocus was how to be highly differentiated from everybody else. We always made sure that we stood out.

Blue Cross Blue Shield of Massachusetts was a big account, and we were competing with Ross Perot's EDS for the business. At the time, we were this tiny little no-name company that was just launching what would be a brand-new product for us, going up against this huge Goliath of a global company. When we showed up at the Blue Cross office in Boston for our final pitch, it happened to be Halloween. So we went out early that morning and bought 40 pumpkins and 30 pounds of candy to hand out to people in the hallway and in our meeting. When we were coming into the building, we had to go up a series of escalators while carrying all these boxes filled with pumpkins and candy. One of the boxes fell over and out spilled the pumpkins. Some of them got jammed in the escalator, and there were pumpkin seeds and juice everywhere. I'm thinking, "Why the hell did we bring all these stupid pumpkins here?" But we picked up the ones that hadn't been engulfed by the jaws of the escalator and persevered. We put on the best show, which made it obvious that we would go the extra mile for customers and really wanted their business. We won the account and it was a game changer for Benefitfocus on many levels.

I was part of the early team that grew Benefitfocus into a very successful company, but then I had a revelation that I wanted to do something different. I took a year off and spent some time in the Bahamas to reflect and work on an idea for a new business in talent management. I needed to disconnect and really plan my thoughts out.

Two epiphanies came to me when I was in the Bahamas. The first was about what I wanted to do with my life. I got a kind of clarity

**PeopleMatter has always been more than a technology company; we are a purpose-driven brand. This is our King Street headquarters the evening we announced our plans for construction in downtown Charleston.**

about my purpose and a vision of what I wanted to do as a human being by mapping my life out into four chapters.

In my first chapter, I wanted to be part of a very successful management team. I wanted to help build a technology start-up from the ground up and take it to great heights. I had already completed that chapter at Benefitfocus.

The second chapter was where I wanted to go next. I realized I wanted to be CEO of a great start-up that could have a meaningful impact on people's lives—the people I worked with and the people we served—a purpose-driven company that would be PeopleMatter.

The third chapter will be about investing in and mentoring other entrepreneurs to help them realize their dreams. I've thought about venture or angel investing and having the opportunity to give back to entrepreneurs and share my war stories, helping them to aspire higher and achieve their dreams.

The final chapter I realized I wanted to complete in my life will be about philanthropic work. I don't yet know what that work will be because it's so far down the road, but I know I want to give back in a meaningful way to a world that has given me so much in my life.

So, that was my first epiphany. My second epiphany was about my next business. I knew I wanted to do something in talent management, because I wanted to apply both my love of technology and my love of relationships with people to a business that I would start myself. There was a lot of momentum in the software industry around talent management at that time and I was seeing a lot of things heating up with some of the big players in the field, including Taleo, SuccessFactors and Kenexa. But, at the same time, I didn't see any company that was really focused on talent management for small to mid-sized businesses. My original business idea was to target those underserved businesses, regardless of industry or subsegment.

Then a friend came to visit and asked me what I was going to do next. I said I was going into talent management for small employers, which I explained as managing the hiring, onboarding, training, engagement and performance of people in a business. He owned several restaurants, so he listened to my ideas and then said, "You have got to do this for the restaurant industry. There are so many opportunities to improve the relationship between the employer and the employee in this industry. Turnover is a pain, and we struggle to find the right people to inspire."

That piqued my interest, so I took a closer look at the restaurant industry and saw an enormous opportunity. I learned that it was the third-largest job creator in the private sector in the United States. I also learned that it was underserved in terms of technology to help employers with managing and developing their people.

But I didn't want to build something just in the restaurant industry, so I looked at other industries that were similar and came up with four: foodservice, hospitality, retail, and what I would call service businesses. The common threads were hourly workers, high turnover, multiple locations, and a high percentage of customer-service roles within the company. That is what inspired me to start PeopleMatter, a company whose purpose would be focused on changing the way the employer and employee interact in the workplace and making it better.

## Starting PeopleMatter

After my time in the Bahamas, I took the lessons I had learned about people to create a vision for PeopleMatter. My early success at Benefitfocus and the customer interactions I'd had working as everything from an ice cream scooper to a car salesman paved my way.

# CUSTOMER SUCCESS STORY

Doublebee's Convenience Stores has seen a radical change in its workforce since it started working with PeopleMatter. The company has even been able to quantify some of the ways it has benefited through hard results, as you can see in the following e-mail from a member of the management team.

......................................

**Date:** January 8, 2013 5:22:16 PM PST
**Subject: BHT PeopleMatter Update**

Guys,

Just wanted to give you an update on our partnership with PeopleMatter.

We hired our first employee on 8-04-12. Since that date we have added 196 employees through your platform.

In Q4 2012 we terminated 91 fewer employees than Q4 2011. Our turnover rate in that timeframe went from 107.21% to 63.46%. A reduction of 43.75%. Not having to train 91 new employees has saved our company well over $20,000 just in training hours for new hires. Our cash shortages in 28 locations were reduced by $10,000. Inventory shrinkage was .67% of inside sales (industry standard is .75%) for the year I have not figured it for Q4 yet but we are extremely pleased with the yearly number. Customer service, clean restrooms overall appearance of our locations, and the other hard to define benefits that come with better employees may be hard to quantify but they are not hard to see with your eyes.

I wanted to sincerely thank everyone there that helped us get to this point. We look forward to a continued partnership with PeopleMatter. Can't wait to shoot you some numbers this time next year.

Thanks,
Doublebee's Convenience Stores

Our product is complete talent management software for service-based employers, which helps them with workforce hiring, onboarding, training, scheduling and communication. But I wanted the company to be about more than just what we do. I looked at books such as *The Progress Principle: Using Small Wins to Ignite Joy, Engagement, and Creativity at Work* by Teresa Amabile and Steven Kramer, and I believed in the principle they talk about, which is that making progress in meaningful work creates an atmosphere in which people are positively engaged in what they do. I knew I wanted us to be a purpose-driven company, but the question was how to make that happen. Early on, I came up with a formula that was really what I would call our engagement and innovation formula: Stimulate + Create = Innovate.

An early logo, taped to the door of our first office. Our company—and brand—have come a long way since 2009.

The first part is "Stimulate," and this means it's the leadership team's job to provide environmental and intellectual stimulation in the form of both the culture and the physical space or atmosphere in which people work. The employees (or team members, as we call them here at PeopleMatter), in turn, bring the "Create" or creative piece. That means hiring people who are creative and passionate about what they do and about doing it well. They have drive. They are engaged. They care about the customers. They want to work hard for their company.

If the leadership team gets that first piece right, the team members will bring this second piece. And the sum of those two parts is what I call "Innovate," which doesn't necessarily mean technological innovation. Rather, it's about how a company stays ahead of its competitors and consistently makes its customers' lives better. I believe this formula can work for any kind of business, whether it's a convenience store, a grocery store, a manufacturer, or a software company.

I also believe it's really important to have a unified vision for an organization and to have a unified team behind that vision, so I brought some spectacular team members on board who believed in these things too. They included Nancy Sansom, whom I had the pleasure of working with for eight years at Benefitfocus and who became our Senior Vice President of Marketing and HR at PeopleMatter. I understood that working with people like her, who shared the same vision and passion for our work, would help us get tremendous traction and results.

We also found our purpose very early on at PeopleMatter, which is to change the way that the employer and employee interact in the workplace and make it better. It's simple and motivating. Our teammates can rally around it and feel empowered to create positive change for the customers we serve.

I wanted to start a company that would blend the benefits of technology with a compassion for people, because that's what the service industry is all about. No other industry relies more on great people and great service for success. I wanted to create solutions that helped service-industry businesses find those great people and get the most out of them. I wanted to change the way they communicate and connect with each other, because then you start to change how people feel about work. You give them purpose. That can really change people's lives.

If you get the right people on your team and really take the time to understand, connect with, and develop them, you have all of these wonderful downstream effects. You'll get greater productivity, better customer service, a more positive workplace, higher sales, lower turnover, and more repeat business. And that's just the beginning. Tons of soft and hard benefits can come out of this.

That is what we do as a company, and that is what I hope this book will do as well.

**The PeopleMatter team in Spring 2011... changing the world and having a blast while doing it!**

# PART 1:

# Why People Matter More Than Ever

**WE ALL KNOW THAT THE ECONOMY** has undergone drastic changes in recent years, and that is especially true for the service-based businesses that we work with at PeopleMatter: restaurants, convenience stores, and other retail businesses. At the same time, our nation's culture has changed and is continuing to do so at a rapid pace, thanks to new technologies and other forces that influence the way we interact with one another. These are things that have a real effect on the way employers run their businesses on a day-to-day basis.

In this section, I want to talk about the changing business landscape that makes it more important than ever to value your people—to engage them, inspire them, take care of them, and communicate with them in ways they are comfortable and familiar with. By doing so, *you can have a positive impact on your business and on the people you work with and serve.*

# CHAPTER 1

# The Disengaged Workforce

**I WAS AT A FLASH FOODS CONVENIENCE STORE** in Waycross, Georgia, when I met a store worker who was an inspirational lady. She had two kids, her husband had left her, and she was working two jobs just to try to make ends meet—one at the convenience store and one at the local Wendy's, as a drive-thru attendant. It can be easy to forget that people in positions like hers have families to provide for and have hopes, dreams and aspirations of their own. The ability to motivate this woman and keep her engaged is, to my mind, one of the most important examples of what we can do here at PeopleMatter.

I believe that people want to feel successful in their work. They want to feel valued. They want to feel that their employers believe they matter and are investing in their success. It's really easy to say that people matter, and when you ask managers or business owners if they believe this, they will say yes almost every time. But do they really? Do they really believe this cashier or that waitress matters? Or do they see people in those positions as functions, as what those people do rather than who they are? And if the employers really do believe that each and every person matters, are they communicating that to their employees frequently?

If you flip the question to employees and ask them whether they feel they matter to their employers, the answer is often a different story. It's amazing what I hear from people who don't even know me when I talk to them in stores. All I usually have to do is ask how they like working there, and a lot of frontline employees will start to discuss various levels of complaints about their employers. Some will be at one extreme, talking about how the job is terrible, how the pay is awful, and how the employer never invests in anyone. Others might be somewhat pleased by their employer but might talk negatively about their colleagues and about how few of them care about their jobs beyond the paycheck they claim each week.

## GALLUP'S DEFINITION OF ENGAGEMENT

Oftentimes there are so many different interpretations of the word *engagement* that it can be difficult to get people to agree on how it's defined. So we'll rely on the definition that Gallup came up with when it conducted its poll, which is that:

- **Engaged employees** work with passion and feel a profound connection to their company. They drive innovation and move the organization forward.

- **Not-engaged employees** are essentially checked out. They're sleepwalking through their workday putting time—but not energy or passion—into their work.

- **Actively disengaged employees** aren't just unhappy at work; they're busy acting out their unhappiness. Every day, these workers undermine what their engaged coworkers accomplish.

Sometimes the nonverbals are just as powerful as the verbals. You look at the body language of those people behind the counter or the cash register and you can see how they feel about being there. Are they smiling? Do they look you in the eye? Are they willing to make an extra effort to get out from behind the counter and help somebody who is looking for something on a shelf? Lots of times the answers to these questions will be "No," "No," and "Are you kidding?" I would describe a lot of service-industry employees today as working on autopilot. These are people who are just there to collect a paycheck. They care nothing about the company beyond that, so they are going to work only the minimum amount they must work to keep their job. Then, as soon as they find a better one, they'll be moving on. On the other hand, I've witnessed some amazing service from employees who are friendly, helpful, engaged, and invested in their work. When you have employees like that, the difference is often palpable from the moment you walk in the door. And that difference often comes back to whether or not people feel that they're being treated well by their employer.

## The State of Disengagement

Disengagement is a one of the latest human resources buzzwords flying around out there, but disengagement in the American workforce isn't a new phenomenon. Gallup does a poll every year to measure employee engagement across industries, and its 2013 *State of the American Workplace* report reveals that 70 percent of workers are "not engaged." The poll also estimates that this widespread disengagement costs the American economy about $550 billion a year. That is a staggering number, which has gotten a good deal of attention, but what's even more concerning is that Gallup has been conducting the same survey for a while now and the number of disengaged employees has been consistent at around 70 percent for more than a decade. With all the latest and greatest training, hiring, motivation and incentive plans out there, one can't help but wonder why we aren't making more progress in engaging our workers. Why aren't employers moving the needle?

Julie Moreland, who is Senior Vice President of our PeopleClues Division at PeopleMatter, has dedicated her career to developing tools that measure job fit, attitude, and engagement levels among employees and job candidates. In her book *Women Who Mean Business*, she wrote about the devastating impact that people who aren't a "good fit" for their jobs (which generally means they're also disengaged) can have on a company:

> Engaged employees in the UK take an average of 2.69 sick days per year; the disengaged take 6.19 (Gallup). And 18 percent of disengaged employees actually undermine their co-workers success (Gallup). But there are other impacts. The worker's family and community also suffer, because the worker is tired and feels trapped in a job that is not a good fit. Everyone is impacted ... the employee, the employer, the team, the family, and the community.

Another negative effect of disengagement is turnover, and this is something that the service industry struggles with even more than most. According to research from the Aberdeen Group, hourly workers have an average turnover rate that is four times higher than that of their exempt counterparts (see sidebars for more on the rates and effect of turnover), and a lot of the companies that PeopleMatter serves today complain about it often. It's a problem that seems to be increasing as the economy continues to recover and grow, which causes employees to change jobs more frequently, pushing up the

Channeling Steve Jobs at the Sept. 14, 2010, launch of our first product, PeopleMatter HIRE™. HIRE drives down turnover, by identifying best-fit applicants and analyzing hiring effectiveness at every level.

turnover rate even more. That's why, as the economy continues to recover, it's more important than ever to engage people in order to retain them.

I learned a lot about the impact turnover has on service-industry companies from Mike Woerner, the Vice President of Human Resources at Thorntons, which is a gasoline and convenience store retailer in the Midwest. Because it can be such a killer for the business, he closely monitors turnover and its effects on his company. When an average team member is working about 30 hours a week, losing even one person puts a lot of pressure on other folks in the store, creates overtime and means management has to spend time and resources hiring and training a new person. That's costly and stressful for the business, so, obviously, employers want to fill the position as quickly as possible.

Time-to-fill is a standard measurement that looks at the number of days it takes to go from when a job opening occurs to when someone is hired for that position. Obviously, companies want that time-to-fill number to be as low as possible. But while time-to-fill measurements give you an idea of the level of burden a company has to bear when it loses employees, Mike once explained to me how he likes to look even deeper into the effects of turnover. In addition to time-to-fill, he looks at how many months or years a terminated employee has been with the company, from the hire date to the date when that employee actually leaves the business. He factors that information in, because in terms of turnover rates, it's a much bigger deal if, say, five people leave this month who had been with the company for three years than if five people leave this month who had been with the company for only six months. In both cases, the turnover rate is the same, but the loss of knowledge and experience is far worse in the first scenario.

Turnover rates and disengagement go hand in hand, because if you have people who don't care about the company and who feel that the company doesn't care about them, why would they stay when a better opportunity comes along? Or, when a friend of theirs says, "You really need to come over here and work at this other company. They treat their people with respect. They pay us a little better. They train us better. The customers are nice, and people like being here." Who wouldn't leave in a situation like that?

In my own career I have seen how a bad environment can really affect people. There is a saying that people leave their managers, not their companies, and I believe that's true. I once worked for a very bright but very difficult boss. Not only did she not appreciate people, but she could also be extremely hard on them, even verbally abusive at times. No employee wants to be around a person like that, no matter how much money that employee is making or how good the job is. Those who stayed became increasingly unhappy and disengaged, and others left as soon as a new opportunity came around.

Experience is obviously one of the best teachers in life and that experience certainly helped me see what not to do when I started my own company, and what I wanted our company to do for both our team members and customers.

The bottom line is that when employees leave a company, their knowledge base—their training, their experience, their passion, the customers they knew and built relationships with—walk out the front door with them. And that has a real impact on the bottom line of any business.

## THE HIGH AND HIDDEN COSTS OF TURNOVER

The Coca-Cola Retailing Research Council found that managerial turnover costs companies $34,735 each time an employee leaves. See the table below for more costs.

| Status | Cost Type | Store Manager | Department Manager | Other Hourly Personnel | Cashier |
|---|---|---|---|---|---|
| Union | Direct | NA | $4,215 | $664 | $584 |
| | Opportunity | NA | $5,749 | $3,627 | $3,729 |
| | Total | NA | $9,964 | $4,291 | $4,313 |
| Nonunion | Direct | $13,936 | $1,658 | $309 | $735 |
| | Opportunity | $20,799 | $5,387 | $3,063 | $1,550 |
| | Total | $34,735 | $7,045 | $3,372 | $2,286 |

## Disengagement: Problem or Opportunity?

There is clearly a fundamental disconnect here: employers saying they care about their people while the vast majority of employees feel

# DOING THE MATH

### The Cost of Turnover for a Housekeeping Attendant

The following shows the cost of turnover for a housekeeping attendant earning $12 an hour, based on the assumption of a two-week notice and a two-week job vacancy.

### Termination costs

| | | |
|---|---|---|
| Separation processing (admin support) | 0.5 hour @ $15/hour | $7.50 |
| Separation processing (management) | 2 hours @ $25/hour | $50 |
| Exit interview (HR staff or consultant) | 1 hour @ $25/hour | $25 |
| Accrued vacation | 5 days | $480 |

### Vacancy/hiring costs

| | | |
|---|---|---|
| Temporary help (wages) | 64 hours @ $12/hour | $768 |
| Writing job ad | | $25 |
| Running job ad | | $75 |
| Application screening | 1.5 hours @ $25/hour | $37.50 |
| Interviewing | 3 hours @ $25/hour | $75 |
| Reference check | 1.5 hours @ $25/hour | $40 |
| Finalizing contract | 0.5 hour @ $25/hour | $12.50 |

### Orientation and training

| | | |
|---|---|---|
| New hire processing | 1 hour @ $15/hour | $15 |
| Orientation | 2 hours @ $25/hour | $50 |
| Orientation materials | | $5 |
| Uniforms/equipment | | $50 |
| In-house training | 12 hours @ $12/hour | $144 |

### Indirect costs

| | | |
|---|---|---|
| Lost productivity of incumbent | 32 hours @ $12/hour | $384 |
| Lost productivity of coworkers | 32 hours @ $12/hour | $384 |
| Lost productivity of supervisor | 18 hours @ $13.50/hour | $243 |
| Lost productivity of new hire during first week | 16 hours @ $12/hour | $192 |
| Lost productivity of new hire in following two weeks | 16 hours @ $12/hour | $192 |
| Increased defects/operating errors | | $50 |
| Dissatisfied or lost customers during transition | | $700 |

### TOTAL TURNOVER COSTS

| | | |
|---|---|---|
| Total direct costs | | $1,859.50 |
| Total indirect costs | | $2,145.00 |
| Total turnover cost | | $4,004.50 |

Source: *Finders & Keepers*, published by Alberta Human Resources and Employment

disengaged and not cared for. And the Gallup numbers suggest that the picture isn't getting any better.

Disengagement is a big problem for employers, but it can also be an opportunity. High rates of disengagement and turnover mean there is room for employers to build better relationships with their employees and to raise their levels of engagement. What's more, they can use this as a point of differentiation from their competitors.

The PeopleMatter Institute (PMI) is a research organization that analyzes industry trends, technologies and tools pertaining to today's hourly workforces. They publish findings that are beneficial for and targeted toward the service industry and are often cited in various trade publications and industry research. PMI's research shows that even basic things such as regular evaluations and performance feedback can make a real difference to employee engagement. (See sidebar for their findings on engagement.) A Gallup poll suggested that the three most important things that employers can do to increase engagement levels are 1) hire the right people (and business consultant and author Jim Collins confirms this critical item as well with his phrase, "Get the right people on the bus!"), 2) develop their strengths, and 3) invest in their well-being.

I will talk more in Part II of this book about specific things you can do to make a difference and drive engagement, including communicating with your people in the way they want to receive communications (which, these days, typically means via technology, especially smartphones.) It also means working to engage people from the start, beginning with their very first contact with the company, before you even hire them. In my opinion, the application process is one of the most important times in the employer-employee relationship, because it sets the tone for how the relationship will evolve. Employers should be asking themselves, "When we are hiring somebody, are we making it easy? Are we communicating well with people throughout the application process? Are we letting them know where they stand?" I have heard lots of candidates say, "I applied for a job, but I don't even know if they got my résumé or application. Is anybody ever going to call me back?" Already, those people feel unappreciated, and you haven't even met them yet.

It's also important to ask yourself how you are representing your brand to prospective new team members. An old-fashioned paper application or poorly built solution using software development language from the 1990s isn't going to inspire people to be excited about your company, especially young workers who make up a large portion of service employees and are so mobile centric and mobile savvy these days.

## ENGAGEMENT FINDINGS FROM PMI'S *HOW HOURLY WORKFORCES WORK* SURVEY

- Forty percent of businesses don't think they do a good job of engaging hourly employees.

- Companies that don't evaluate hourly employees' performance are three times more likely to report turnover rates greater than 100 percent.

- Companies using a workforce management system (WMS) to track and record employee performance are nearly twice as consistent in providing regular performance feedback.

- Companies that regularly and consistently provide performance feedback are two times less likely to report 100 percent-plus turnover than those who provide feedback annually and inconsistently.

We use our own hiring software to recruit, screen and onboard new PeopleMatter team members. It makes a great first impression on our applicants and helps us hire and onboard the best ones quickly.

These are examples of opportunities for engagement even before someone starts working for your company. The people you hire have started to form an idea of how they will be treated in your workplace even before they show up for their very first day of work. And what about all the people you don't hire? Those are potential customers or future referral sources for your company. You have to ask yourself what sort of impression you've made on them through your application and hiring processes. Is it one that gives them a positive impression of you and your brand? Or is it one that leaves them with a negative view of your business? (More on this subject in Chapter 4, "The Science behind the Art of Hiring.")

## Laggards versus Innovators

Two groups of companies are emerging in the service industry today. There are the progressive innovators, which are companies that focus on their culture and how to increase employee engagement. I would include in that category a number of companies that I have learned from, such as Thorntons, Roadrunner Markets, MAD Greens, Wildflower Bread Company, and Noodles & Company, among others. These companies are out there, constantly looking for ways to improve their workforce culture and understand the direct relationship between a valued employee and the bottom line of their business.

Then you have the group of laggards who don't do these things. It's not necessarily that they don't want to or they don't believe these things would add value, but, most likely, they are just caught up in the day-to-day challenges of running their businesses. So they are not investing in their culture. They are not investing in new tools. They still look at their people in the same way that companies did 20 or 30 years ago, which is that employees are just there to do a job and little more is required from the company beyond giving them a paycheck. These laggards are stuck in the past and are not making the necessary technological and cultural changes that they need to make in order to succeed in the future.

I believe the laggards are going to continue to decline in key metrics and lose sales and customers in the coming years because they are not innovating or investing. The innovators are going to attract the best people. Newer, younger workers are going to gravitate toward the innovators, because they want to work for a company that cares about them and invests in and believes in a strong culture where employees are appreciated. And, most importantly, young workers have technological expectations and will lean toward companies that use technology to help them drive that engagement.

## THE IMPORTANCE OF PEOPLE TO THE BOTTOM LINE

"It's really our people who help impact sales. We're a traditional convenience store chain. That means you can buy a 20-ounce Mountain Dew or a bag of chips or a six-pack of beer. But you can buy all those things at a multitude of other places, including other convenience stores, drugstores and grocery stores. So where we have to set ourselves apart is operationally and that means having great customer service. That's the only thing we can do to differentiate ourselves from the guy across the street, because he sells Mountain Dew and Frito-Lays just like we do."

**—Ryan Broyles, President and CEO, Roadrunner Markets**

## Making a Difference

When it comes to engaging employees, there are real, attainable goals that can make a big difference to your business and to the lives of the people who work for you. When I visited that convenience store in Georgia, I could tell that our product had really changed things for that single mom who was working behind the counter. Her employer had invested in training for her, and she felt more empowered and more in control as a result. I think back to when I worked at Swensen's Ice Cream as a kid. It could have been a boring job, but the manager engaged the entire team of employees and gave us the information we needed to succeed in our positions. I was trained to ask every customer, "Do you want a cup or a cone, one scoop or two scoops, and what flavor?" Just knowing the right questions to ask and being empowered with that knowledge makes the employee feel more prepared and more confident. This will affect the customer experience.

I think a lot of people who are not empowered with information feel marginalized, so they cut corners and will not go out of their way to help a customer out. If they know more about their jobs, if they know more about the specials and the opportunities to up-sell and how that impacts the company, if they understand how they can help the company succeed and meet or beat its revenue goals, if they understand how meeting those goals affects their opportunities for continued employment and advancement, then they will do a better job. They will do a better job because they feel prepared and have more pride in their workplace. That is what I saw with that single mom. Just connecting those dots for her made her a happier employee. It also made her a more efficient and effective employee, because she understood the benchmarks of success.

What so many employees want is appreciation and communication in the workplace. I really believe that. I think they want to know how to do their jobs better, and they want to be highlighted and thanked when they are doing a great job. The good news for employers is that it's easy to give employees that confirmation, and everyone ends up benefiting as a result.

# CHAPTER 2

# The New Economy

**DISENGAGEMENT, AS I MENTIONED** in the last chapter, has been a problem for American employers for more than a decade. But it's becoming more and more important that businesses have people who are invested in their work and want to stick around. That's because the workforce landscape has changed dramatically in recent years, and it is continuing to change, a fact that has a real day-to-day impact on employers, particularly in service-industry businesses. There are macroeconomic forces at work, for sure. The Affordable Care Act and immigration reform are already affecting businesses and will continue to do so in new ways. The uncertainty with Congress and government infighting has been hard on a lot of employers. And the effects of the 2008 economic downturn are still being felt in a lot of sectors, especially the service industry.

Those are some of the big economic drivers that are affecting businesses in the United States today, but they are not the only changes underway. At the same time, technological developments are changing the way people interact and communicate with one another. These forces affect our culture as a whole, but service-industry businesses feel them even more keenly than most due to the demographics and makeup of their typical workforces.

You can see some of these changes at work in the way companies are embracing new relationships with their workers. The numbers of freelancers, independent contractors, part-time workers, and employees with flexible work schedules are all on the rise. For example, according to the Freelancers Union, nearly one-third of the American workforce—or 42 million workers—are considered independent workers today. And that number is growing. Freelancers are expected to make up a full 40 percent of the workforce by 2020. In the service industry, as well as others, some companies are adapting to rising health-care costs and other economic factors by shifting to more part-time workers, which means managing more people who are working fewer hours. Companies are making these changes because it allows them to cut costs and work more efficiently.

The way employers react to these fundamental shifts in our economy will have a lot to do with whether or not they will be successful. I talked in the last chapter about laggards versus innovators when it comes to engagement, and the same divide applies here as well. Innovative companies are adapting to these changing forces in the economy and finding new opportunities to improve the way they do business. Laggards continue with business as usual and their companies are likely to pay for it.

Wally Doolin is the Chairman of TDn2K (Turning Data into Knowledge), a company that he founded with his wife Joni and that studies these kinds of economic shifts and the impact they have on the restaurant industry, in particular. As a former chain restaurant operator, Wally has been part of the restaurant business since the early 1970s and has seen a lot of changes firsthand. As he put it, "We experienced about 30 years of growth in our industry, fueled by a great economy and trends like women entering the workforce and the rise of two-income families. That continued until about the mid-2000s, which was when growth flattened out. We're at a point in time now when the industry has reached maturity, so today it's a market share battle." That makes it even more crucial that businesses do things to differentiate themselves as they compete for both customers and employees, things such as hiring the right people and having the right processes in place for onboarding and training.

## OPPORTUNITIES TO ATTRACT EMPLOYEES

People Report notes that the average restaurant company offers the perks listed below. For those looking to attract better talent, offering more than the norm in one of these areas is a way that businesses can really set themselves apart from their competitors.

The average restaurant company offers its employees:

- zero paid sick, holiday, or personal days;

- four paid vacation days after one year of tenure, and seven days at five years;

- twenty-seven percent of companies offer free dining;

- eighty-six percent offer dining discounts;

- twenty-nine percent offer some form of education assistance;

- only 19 percent offer flexible scheduling ← **a huge opportunity, since hourly workers are looking for this.**

Among the changes he has seen in the industry is more workforce diversification, both in terms of ethnicity and age. A couple of decades ago, quick-service restaurant (QSR) employees were mostly teens and young adults, but according to People Report (a part of TDn2K which provides human resource metrics, benchmarks, trends and best people practices for the food-service industry), the average age of QSR employees today is about 26. The industry is also hiring more part-time workers and that number, according to Wally, is likely to go up even more, given the macro forces at work we discussed earlier.

These changes would be challenging enough in good times, but Wally points out that the restaurant industry still hasn't recovered fully from the economic downturn. People Report's research suggests that people who eat out still aren't doing it as often as they used to, and some are trading down in the type of restaurant they visit. Wally's team tracked about 16,000 restaurant units and found that these businesses are still about five percentage points behind where they were in 2008 in terms of comparable sales and about 8 percent behind in terms of traffic.

"The restaurants tightened their belt, like all businesses did to get through the downturn," Wally explained. "They got through it, but now what? You can't get more efficient unless you apply technology. So, one of the big things we talk about in our organization is how to leverage technology to get greater efficiency." It is one of the greatest opportunities going today for transforming your business.

Even though the restaurant business is well known for its high turnover rates and low margins, Wally points out that there are "people in all categories of a business that really dramatically out-perform their peers." To call attention to that idea, his company started handing out annual Best Practices Awards. "These awards kind of blow up some of the assumptions about the industry," Wally explained, "like the idea that fast food businesses can't be good at retention. White Castle has won the Best Practices Award five times in the QSR category, and its retention rate has outpaced all other categories several times. This company has been around for 90 years!

It isn't just the newest and the coolest concepts that retain talent. It is leadership utilizing systems, process, and genuine caring that holds onto the best talent."

## John Sumser on Technology and the New Economy

John Sumser is a guru in the HR technology world. He is the founder, principal author, and editor-in-chief of the *HRExaminer*, a weekly online human resources magazine, and he is the principal of Two Color Hat, where he routinely advises teams on issues relating to human resources, recruiting and talent management. Plus, he is a member of the PeopleMatter Board of Advisors and believes, as I do, that technology already plays—and is going to continue to play—a tremendous role in the new economy in terms of employee recruitment, development, retention and growth.

Here is just some of what I've learned from John, in his own words:

I am 59 years old and generally, people my age don't get the notion that work is supposed to be fun. I think that's sort of a generational difference between the baby boomers and the people who follow along behind them. So why is work supposed to be fun and engaging? The reason is that work is where people go today to get a sense of belonging. Families are small and disconnected. The media doesn't provide a narrative the way it used to. In the new economy, people go to work, and they don't make the separation between home and work. It's all the same thing and social media has really accelerated that.

I recently had what I thought was kind of a strange inter-action with a young marketing guy. His idea was that there was something wrong with an HR department that didn't treat its employees the same way the company treated its customers. He was furious because HR treated people as actual human resources rather than people. That's a view that's hard for us old-school people to under-stand. The idea that an employee has a meaning and a right to be treated like a human being rather than like

**When you talk about engaging somebody, what you really mean is you want all of that person on the job, because that's how you get better results from an employee.**

a widget that goes on the assembly line—that's probably the fundamental difference between the old economy and the new economy.

But that's a bigger bundle of stuff to deal with because people come with weird preferences and different tastes in music and from odd family backgrounds. When you try to get your arms around that whole thing, it seems wildly complicated and horribly difficult if you're used to dealing with widgets.

That's why some foodservice franchises are hitting man-agement problems. The very nature of management changes when you have active participants in the enter-prise rather than people who just fit the job descriptions and perform roles. They're people who need to be able to talk to each other and who want to be able to easily change their schedules and choose to work with people they want to work with, or not work with people they don't want to work with. If you want to build an enterprise that's based on that kind of fundamental choice for the employee, it takes a different mindset.

I don't know that it's actually harder to do it this way, but if you've been managing people like widgets for 30 years and somebody comes along and says you've got to manage them like they're your kids or your next-door neighbor, it's a hard transition to make and not everybody can make it gracefully.

When I first started thinking about this stuff, I had a gut reaction. I was a classic manager from big companies, and the idea that somebody who worked for me was supposed to like their job seemed completely off. Why should I care if they like their job or not? I pay them, after all. But the movement, the employee face of the new economy, is all about the desire to feel like you're in the middle of something. You go to work and there's a narrative unfolding of what's going on in the restaurant or of this project that you're doing. You could trivialize it and say it's about a sense of belonging, but it's deeper than that. Work is becoming the source of meaning in many peoples' lives. That's a wild idea.

There is this really cool thing about human beings and technology, and that is that just as the problem arises, the technology comes along to solve it. You can see this happening over and over again throughout history. Today technology enables you to make the work environment more accommodating to people, while also being clearer about what you're trying to get done. People find it easier to do what needs to be done and they find it easier to be in an environment where belonging is central.

The other thing that happens is that people integrate that technology into their work lives. So the question that you have ask is whether it is okay for the hostess in a restaurant to be on her cell phone checking Facebook. Is that a good thing or is that a bad thing?"

Old-school managers will instantly tell you that's a terrible thing; you should never have the hostess on her cell phone checking Facebook. But managers who are doing well in this new environment will say, "Well, you know what? If we don't have anything to do, why should she have to stand there and do nothing? What she needs to be able to do is switch between the clever way she's occupying her time when there's nothing to do and putting down her phone when a customer walks in." I mean, what people on restaurant staffs do is wait. So, if you can find a way to stay occupied in the present tense while you're waiting, which is a large part of the job, it's a really good thing. But that is really hard to adjust to if you are an old-school manager. You paid people to wait. You paid people less than minimum wage to wait. You tried to get them to go home if they had to wait too much. Understanding this takes a different mindset.

## Millennials in the Workforce

Another piece of this puzzle is that the millennial generation, which is roughly defined as the generation born between 1980 and 2000, is entering the workforce in increasing numbers. These workers will make up about 75 percent of the U.S. workforce by 2025 and are big drivers in this new economy. The thing about this generation of young people is that their view of the workplace is different. They expect a lot of engagement, feedback and communication. They are also more technologically savvy and expect to communicate via technology. They expect to receive text messages when their schedule changes, for example. This is a new way of working for some managers, but it also gives employers an opportunity to reach employees through their employees' preferred method of communication.

Another thing that is different about millennials is they expect to have a path for growth that is clearly defined, and they expect to get promoted quickly. Research supports this, and we see it every day in our workplace, where young people come in and want to move to a different role or up in the organization in as little as six months! Maybe they're not ready, but they expect to move or they will move on to another company. We call it the millennial flare-up, and we kind of joke among the management team that these young people want to be CEO within a year.

Nancy Sansom is PeopleMatter's Senior Vice President of Marketing and she has seen this over and over again. As she explains, "I've done hundreds of interviews as a hiring manager, and when I interview millennials and ask them why they are leaving their current job, one of the commonest things they will tell me is, 'I don't know what's next for me.' That is a huge theme for them. Now that's also a fairly safe reason to give in an interview, and I think the other big reason is that they don't like their manager, which usually means a lack of engagement, but that's more difficult to say in an interview. But the number-one reason given in an interview is, 'I don't know where my career path is leading.' Sometimes I'll ask if they have talked to their manager about it, but, typically, they don't see that as their responsibility."

## THE MILLENNIAL VIEW

According to a CareerBuilder.com survey, 56 percent of millennials expect a promotion within a year. At the same time, more than 80 percent of hiring managers believe that this group has a stronger sense of entitlement than other workers.

Millennials tend to expect their company and their manager to tell them where their career path is heading and to help them get there. Our way of addressing that at PeopleMatter is to have a defined career path, a published career path that our millennial employees know about and that offers pretty frequent movement but is based on results. Instead of saying that in six months you're going to move, we say that once you've achieved a certain result, you have the opportunity to move to the next step in your career. This is how you can kind of bridge the gap between what your management team needs, which are results, and what the millennials want, which is growth and direction. And this is something that companies across the board could be a lot better at.

When we want to celebrate a big milestone, we fire a cannon; a real, live 150-year-old cannon. The cannon—and Keith, the man who helps us fire it—are a fun, unique part of our culture now.

Millennials also want, even expect, a different kind of culture in the workplace than we've had in the past. Another way we bridge that gap at PeopleMatter is that we show our appreciation for people and the good work they do. We recognize people in front of the entire company every week. We do these things called patio meetings, which I learned while at Benefitfocus. They are weekly meetings where we spend 30 minutes giving an update on the business, and then we recognize two or three people for having done an outstanding job during the prior week and for embodying our core values. This helps us reinforce our core values. We do that weekly with over 150 people, and I know other companies do it, as well. LinkedIn does an all-hands meeting every other week for thousands of employees. InsideSales.com has weekly meetings, and Wal-Mart is famous for its Saturday-morning meetings, which Sam Walton started when the company was just getting going.

## FINDINGS FROM PMI'S *HOW HOURLY WORKFORCES WORK* SURVEY

- Defining career paths and goals is 73 percent easier when using a workforce management system versus paper/manual processes.

- Companies that allow employees to view and manage schedules online are 28 percent more efficient in controlling labor costs than those that don't.

- Companies that offer advancement opportunities are 25 percent more efficient at providing great customer service than those that don't.

- These companies are also 2.3 times less likely to report turnover rates greater than 100 percent than those that don't provide career paths.

We also make sure to highlight peer-to-peer recognition. Ours comes in the form of a bobble-head doll called Mr. Fantastic that team members award to one another each week. I love hearing about the day-to-day things our team members are doing and seeing the huge impacts those things are having on our culture, our customers and our efficiency.

Showing your employees you appreciate them doesn't have to be complicated or a big production. We've found a little beer and socializing can go a long way. We even went so far as to literally build this notion into our building. Our rooftop patio has three beer taps, and we encourage our team members to go up anytime. We even have a beer-by-democracy election whereby each floor gets to vote for which beers are on tap. Not all business owners can crack open a six-pack with their employees, and I certainly don't mean it's the answer every time, but it does foster community and communication in a way that our team members, particularly our millennial team members, really relate to. And some really great ideas have come out of these impromptu conversations—conversations that probably never would have happened otherwise. It all goes back to Stimulate + Create = Innovation. If you make sure employees have a place to relax, blow off steam and connect with each other (stimulate), they're going to be happier (create more good stuff) and they're going to perform better (keep innovating).

The point is that there are always ways to get together and share information, regardless of how big the company is. And in this new economy, workers are coming to expect things such as weekly meetings, recognition, and regular feedback and communication, preferably via technology, more and more.

# PART II:

# Action Items–
# How to Put People First

**IN THE LAST SECTION,** we looked at why, in this new economy, you should view your people as more important than ever to the success of your business. Changing cultural and economic factors, along with technological advancements, present new opportunities for understanding, managing and motivating your workforce and for breaking away from the competition.

Now that you understand the *why* behind the idea that people matter, it's time to put that idea into practice. This second section provides action items, simple things you can do in your company to put people first. In doing so, you can make a real difference in the lives of your people, as well as in the success of your business.

## CHAPTER 3

# Think Differently about People

**THE FIRST STEP TOWARD** making sure people really do matter in your business is to shift your mindset from thinking of employees as human doings to thinking of them as human beings. In the service industry in particular, but in other businesses as well, old perceptions of the labor force persist: people are seen as little more than their functions—as in, that's just a cashier or a waiter. You can hear it in the language people use, for example, "I need *bodies* on the floor." But it's important to keep in mind that an employee in your company, no matter the position, is an individual who has goals, who has meaning and who wants to have a purpose in life.

Instead of only thinking about what our employees do for us, we can start thinking about how we can enrich the lives of our workforce or how we can make the workplace a better place for them. To do that, you have to start with your culture and establish an environment in which people are seen as whole beings.

Creating the right culture usually starts with your mission, vision, purpose and values. I've found that most companies have some, but not all, of these elements. If I were to rank them in order of most to least common, I would say that number one, most companies have a vision of where they want to go. Then, quite a few have a mission statement as well. A distant third is the number of companies that have clearly articulated their values. And then, rarely, they will have the fourth piece, which is their purpose or their why. Why do they do what they do? That's the purpose a company needs to identify first. I think far too many companies lack a purpose and a set of values. In my mind, these are the two most important pieces, particularly the purpose, because that is what will inspire owners and employees to come to work each and every day.

## What—How—Why

I believe that if you want to think differently about people, you have to map out what that means. An easy model to use is one that has worked for us at PeopleMatter and for many others, which is the what-how-why model.

Back in 2010 I watched a video of a TED talk by Simon Sinek on how great leaders inspire action. It's been viewed more than 15 million times, and it's a great 18-minute video clip that I highly recommend any leader watch. It talks about the what, the how, and the why of a company—what they do, how they do it, and why they do what they do. (You can also check out Sinek's book *Start With Why: How Great Leaders Inspire Everyone to Take Action*, for more on these ideas.)

The *what* is asking what you do: What business are you in? Are you in the convenience store business? Are you in the retail business? What do you serve? What actions do you take in your business?

To give you an example, our *what* here at PeopleMatter is we build workforce management software for service-based employers. We help companies in high-turnover, customer-service-focused, multilocation environments with workforce hiring, training, scheduling and performance management. Another way of looking at it is we provide HR in the cloud for the service industry. That is our *what*.

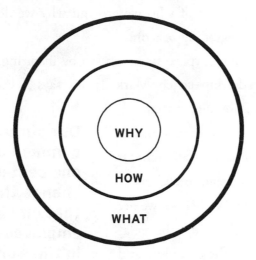

The *how* is asking how you do it. The *how* for us is that we are a software-as-a-service (SaaS) company, which is a software model that is hosted in the cloud and delivered through the Internet and mobile devices. We have an agile scrum process that allows us to be flexible and release new features frequently, which, for us, is at least four times a year. That gives our customers the benefit of getting new updates and enhancements on a regular basis. We also have two sales teams. We have what we call a core sales team that focuses on small to mid-size employers, and a national account team that focuses on large enterprise employers. So, to sum up, our *how* is that we have an agile development process and a software methodology delivered through the Internet and mobile devices, which we sell to customers through two separate sales forces.

Most companies have defined their *what* and their *how*, but their *why*, the inner circle, is the most important part. It's also the part that's most often overlooked. The *why* is your purpose, and our purpose at PeopleMatter is very simple. It's summed up in one sentence: *to change the way that employers and employees interact in the workplace and to make it better.* I put that in bold because it really gets at the heart of who we are and why we do what we do every day. It's our guiding beacon.

You want your purpose statement to be inspiring. As my close friend and leadership coach Mark Tribus says, "The capacity to embrace something bigger than self is what draws people to a common goal." Our purpose statement is what inspires our team members to do what they do. We believe we are fundamentally changing the relationship between the employer and employee through a piece of technology that enables communication

**Our purpose is summed up in one sentence: to change the way that employers and employees interact in the workplace and to make it better.**

and engagement and that streamlines a lot of cumbersome processes. That allows for a lot of downstream effects to take place in the businesses we serve, and those effects include happier customers, more repeat sales, and more upsells. Customers are spending more in the businesses that use our technology, because when they visit the stores or restaurants, they enjoy the employees they interact with. And employees stay longer in these companies, because they have better relationships with their employer, which makes them happier overall.

It's worth noting that our purpose statement is all about people, not technology, even though that's the field we're in. I believe that makes a real difference in how our people view their jobs. As Mark Deaton, our former Senior Vice President of Customer Care and one of the best customer service leaders I have had the opportunity to work alongside, said, "I don't really think of us as a technology company. I think of us as a service company that happens to use technology to provide that service. I think it's sort of built into the DNA at PeopleMatter that we're a service provider first."

It can take some time to get your purpose right, but I really believe it's worth spending time on because it's a huge part of how you can motivate and inspire your people. And, as we learned in previous chapters, motivation and inspiration are things that too many employees lack these days. If everyone in your company understands their *why*—why it's so important that I get up, go to work, and do my best job at this company every day to impact the lives of the customers we serve—that will unleash a lot of opportunities for growth in your business.

Our logo on a huge 37 by 16 foot banner, hanging high atop our not-yet-finished world headquarters building. It's a powerfully simple logo that speaks to both our company and our purpose.

## Communicating Your *Why*

Another big piece of the puzzle is the effective communication of your *why*, or purpose. A lot of employers will do one of two things after they do the work of coming up with their *why*: They will do absolutely nothing to communicate it, or they will do very little—

maybe some orientation training or they will throw the language up on their website or on a wall somewhere in a hallway and hope that employees take the time to look at it. What you see in companies that have done a great job of grounding their organizations on their *why* is that the message is clear and constantly reinforced.

A great way to consistently reinforce your *why* is through technology. Our learning module, for example, is a great platform for embedding that *why* into the training courses that people take. I also think it takes a commitment among the leadership to keep beating that drum within the organization and communicating the *why* each and every day.

## Purpose-Driven Companies

I had the good fortune of meeting Louis Basile, President and CEO of Wildflower Bread Company, at a National Restaurant Association annual meeting several years ago. I was immediately excited and captivated by what he had to say about the purpose and vision of his company.

Wildflower's purpose statement is very easy to understand and communicate: "We change lives, create traditions, build community and feed the soul with passion. Every time, every day!" That says far more than your standard company mission statement. It's very aspirational, and it motivates the company's people to aim higher in what they do.

You get a sense of this purpose the moment you walk into one of the company's restaurants. You can just feel the culture and the passion employees have for what they're doing and for the people they interact with. I visit a lot stores around the country, and I can often feel the opportunities for improvement right when I walk in the door. It doesn't take much to enter a store and, in the first two minutes, get a sense of what that organization is all about or what it's not about. You walk around and can tell pretty quickly how people are being treated and whether or not the company is inspiring and taking care of them. What is really remarkable is when I get to visit a store before it becomes a customer and then after it has used the PeopleMatter Platform™. I get to see noticeable differences among the workforce, from happier employees to happier customers, which motivates us to keep building great software.

An interesting tactic that Louis used to put his people first is he made them part of the process of coming up with the company's purpose and values. Instead of mandating the purpose and values by himself or with his management team and then just telling everyone what they were, he put together a diverse group of Breadheads called the Slice Team (Breadheads are what they call the people who work at Wildflower), took them to an offsite location, and provided a forum and process for them to develop Wildflower's purpose and values together. Louis knew it would be the right purpose when everyone in the room agreed. As Louis explained: "We took Breadheads who had been with us for years, as well as some who were relatively new to the company. We took hourly and salary Breadheads. We had someone representing all the pieces of the business at the table. The meeting was supposed to end on a Friday afternoon and as it got closer to that time, we thought we were done. I figured everyone wanted to get home for the weekend, and then a new Breadhead who worked in our manufacturing facility raised his hand and said, 'I'm not 100 percent sure that our work is complete.' That led to an additional hour or two of discussion and, ultimately, agreement, and that's how we ended up with such a bold purpose statement."

"I'll always remember that moment," Louis told me, "because

those are the gems. To see someone like that finding his confidence and inner voice and then to step outside his comfort zone by raising his hand and speaking up was really impactful for me."

The same group came together and developed the company's values. "I think it took us three different meetings—over about five or six days of really intense conversations and debates—to come up with our 11 values," Louis said. "It wasn't easy, and, at the same time, it was so important because our values are the railroad tracks that keep us on the right path, always heading toward our purpose."

# Inspirational Messages from Companies that Put People First

## WILDFLOWER BREAD COMPANY

### Our Purpose
We change lives, create traditions, build community and feed the soul with passion. Every time, every day.

### Our Values
We change lives, create traditions, build community and feed the soul with passion. Every time, every day:

> by honoring and preserving the art of making world class bread.
>
> by being passionate about service and great food.
>
> by appreciating and caring for each other as family.
>
> by positively impacting and strengthening our community and planet.
>
> by consciously practicing self-awareness and embracing opportunities to grow.
>
> by ensuring excellence through continuous education.
>
> by being accountable for our choices, commitments and actions.
>
> by communicating everything openly, honestly and respectfully.
>
> by actively seeking and sharing knowledge to improve.
>
> by celebrating innovation.
>
> by delivering revered financial results.

# ST. ROMAIN OIL

St. Romain Oil is a family-owned convenience store and wholesale fuels company, proudly and locally operating for three generations. Our mission is to refuel and refresh the communities of Louisiana, surprising our customers' appetites with fast, freshly prepared food.

As a family-owned business, we value:

**Service:** We are committed to serving our communities by being available: open 24/7. During emergencies, we're the last to close and the first to open, providing our guests with fuel, food and merchandise to meet their convenience needs.

**Community:** We are committed to building the communities we serve through local employment and a strong and active local presence.

**Integrity:** We care deeply that our guests, our team members, and our business partners should always be treated with honesty and respect.

**Pioneering:** We believe in pursuing success and are always striving to improve what we offer and how we deliver it to our guests.

**Teamwork:** We strive to be a quality employer of quality people and are committed to their well-being and career development.

**Success:** We are dedicated to providing competitively priced quality products and quick, friendly service to our guests in clean and safe stores.

........................||||||||||||

# SWEETGREEN

Founded in 2007, Sweetgreen is a destination for delicious food that's both healthy for you and aligned with your values. We source local and organic ingredients from farmers we know and partners we trust, supporting our communities and creating meaningful relationships with those around us. We exist to create experiences where passion and purpose come together.

**Core Values**
These five core values embody our culture, spirit and dedication to doing what's right. They keep us aligned and help us make decisions

about everything, from the food we serve to the way we design our stores:

- win, win, win—create solutions in which the company wins, the customer wins, the community wins;

- think sustainably—make decisions that will last longer than you will;

- keep it real—cultivate authentic food and relationships;

- add the sweet touch—create meaningful connections everyday from farm to patron:

- make an impact—think smarter, work harder, do it together.

...................................

# FAMILY EXPRESS

**Our Mission**
We provide our customers with total satisfaction by offering competitively priced, high-quality products and services, in a clean, safe and friendly environment. We serve our community through volunteerism and we are profitable in order to assure the future prosperity of our employees and our company.

**Our Vision**
To be the finest small chain of convenience stores and fueling centers in the world.

Family Express is recognized in the market place by its passion for customer service. The company has engineered itself in the art of building relationships with its customers by utilizing its "living brand." Family Express's living brand is its uniquely friendly employees.

...................................

## BOLOCO

Our mission is to better the lives and futures of our people. We use ridiculously delicious burritos to do it. And it's literally the most important thing we do.

We believe that even a burrito aspires. We know. It's hard to take a burrito this seriously. Super hard. And don't worry. You don't have to. That's our job.

You just need to love what we do. If ever we fail to inspire or delight, let us know. We'll make it right.

The Boloco philosophy is to be appealingly off-center (i.e., never boring!), to not take ourselves too seriously, and to strive for 100 percent honesty even when it hurts. While we absolutely love that our culture is one in which we consistently go overboard to amaze our guests, to make up for mistakes and generally shock and awe those who visit us, our main focus is on positively impacting the lives and future of our people.

..................................

# Think Differently about Yourself as a Leader

Thinking differently or creating a mindset shift isn't easy, no matter what the topic. I think we all need people around us who challenge us and help us see things and do things in a new way. Louis of Wildflower Bread Company has been one of those people for me. In the years since we first met, he has become both a customer and a close friend. He is somebody who is always challenging me and pushing me to build better products and services and to look at things in new ways. That has made me a better leader and made our company a better company.

As John Sumser explained in Chapter 2, the idea that we should be thinking differently about our people by putting them first is a relatively new idea in the world of work. And even if we believe this in theory, that doesn't mean that we don't fall back on old habits or ingrained ways of thinking. Any kind of change needs to start with self-knowledge and owning who you are. Mark Tribus is an expert on building authentic communities, cohorts and winning teams, and he has coached me, personally, as well as my executive team members, to become more effective and more authentic leaders.

Each year, we host a big customer meetup called Collaborate; it's a great way to connect with our customers and we get incredible product ideas and feedback.

Here is just some of what Mark has taught me about authentic leadership:

Everybody wants to know that they're worthy and that they have something to contribute, but cultures inside organizations can be unauthentic and even toxic at times, where the norm becomes sizing each other up with scorecards and personal advancement at the expense of others. People would say, "Well, that's how a capitalistic society works."

I would say, "Yeah, it does, but it doesn't have to be done in such a malicious, self-interested manner. *Teams* can do better."

There is a more open and authentic way, but it takes work and it's not always typical or natural. What is natural is to protect our identities and our own insecurities. It takes a real leader who has the capacity to be completely wide open and vulnerable to say, "Hey, I'm going to accept these people for who they are, with all their strengths and areas for development." But it's absolutely game changing when you spend the time and energy to see each unique human being in your business rather than just the business. It requires more of a leader's insight, care and compassion, but in the end, it's game changing in terms of how those people perform inside the organization. "Do you see an office or 40 uniquely talented women and men? Do you see a company or 250 gifted and special teammates?

I have worked with a lot of teams to build and enhance trust, because it's the glue of any great team. People talk about trust all the time, but we don't really know what trust is. The gateway to trust is through vulnerability, and it's counterintuitive in our society to be vulnerable at work when we can get "hurt" because of self-interested or ego-driven behavior. So we pretend a lot to protect our sense of self-worth. But the reality is that when you can open up and be authentic, amazing things, transformative things, can happen on teams. And when you're not authentic, when you don't own your weaknesses and you pretend as a leader, people know it and it gives your employees license to pretend as well and to hide their own weaknesses. Because, if you're my leader and you don't acknowledge your weaknesses—maybe you have a tendency to cut people off, to be very short with them, to curse at times—then that gives me license as your subordinate to pretend about my own areas of weakness. Now we're both pretending and six months down the road, you are looking at me and wondering why I couldn't accomplish a task to your standard. You're wondering why I didn't tell you that I didn't know how to do something or that my project was off track. But I pretended because I saw you pretending and I was afraid to be honest with you about what I didn't know. In the end, there's a pretty clear business case to be made that when we all pretend in a company, it hurts the business. Wouldn't you, as a leader, rather have someone who feels comfortable coming to you and saying, "I don't know what I'm doing"? That way, you can help them out or find someone else who does know what they're doing without wasting time or effort.

Everybody wants to go to work every day and feel good about what they do. In many organizations, this is not the case. Instead, people are protective of themselves and hang onto what they have, versus going there to fully contribute knowing that it's a safe place just to be themselves. You have to build a safe container for people so they can show up and feel free to be who they are—including all the good, the bad and the ugly. And that starts with the leader being authentic.

To give an example, I did peer assessments with the leadership team at PeopleMatter where everyone gave each other feedback. Everyone was assessed on sixteen different dimensions, which are things like how this person appears to other people, what their orientation to winning is, and how well they receive feedback. The feedback is all anonymous, and then I compile it into a one-page feedback form for each person.

There was one member of the PeopleMatter team who got back her feedback form and it showed some areas that she needed to work on, or "blind spots," including how she accepted feedback. So I said to her, "I challenge you to take this feedback page and, at your next senior management meeting, hand a copy of it to everybody on the team who assessed you." She did it. She handed the page to everyone and said, "Thank you for the feedback. I own this behavior, and if you see me do any of these things again, I hope you'll hold me accountable." Feedback is a *gift*.

## Thinking Differently Creates Change

It may seem a little bit odd to some that I started off this section of the book, which is supposed to be about action items, not by talking about how to act differently but about how to think differently. But this kind of different thinking, this kind of mindset shift, is the first step toward creating real, significant changes in your business.

John Pepper, who is one of the founders and the former CEO of the Boston-based burrito chain Boloco, said that when he and his partner first started the business, it was really the product they were focused on, not the people. John was still in business school at the time and had recently lived in San Francisco, where he became what he calls a "burrito fanatic," and that's what inspired him to open a restaurant.

## Tool: Understanding How Your Weaknesses Benefit You

**by Mark Tribus**

Being aware of our self-protective behaviors doesn't mean they go away. People always say to me, "Mark, this thing is such a weakness of mine," as if they can't help but do it. But in reality, it's not a weakness. That's not the problem. I always reply, "If a weakness were like drinking gasoline, you wouldn't do it. You act the way you act because in some way it actually serves you."

If people say that doesn't make sense, I say, "If interrupting and cutting people off in meetings were like drinking gasoline, you wouldn't do it, so, obviously you do it for some reason." People often reply, "Well, Mark, I can't think of a good reason why interrupting and cutting people off is a good thing." I say, "Well, I can think of lots of reasons. You get to have your say. You keep the conversation short. You don't have to listen to what others have to say or their opinions. In many ways, cutting people off and interrupting does serve you. That's probably why you do it."

But then I remind people, "It can also sting you because behaviors like that just don't work well with people or on a *team*. They don't build trust and they don't help you work as a team. So, interrupting and cutting somebody off also stings you as well as it serves you."

His new outlook developed during Boloco's second year of business, while he was mopping the floor one night. An employee hadn't shown up for his shift, so John was forced to stay late on a Saturday night to close the restaurant, missing a big party of his business school friends in the process. As he begrudgingly moved that mop across the restaurant floor, he realized something, which was that "mopping sucks." That, in turn, made him start to question a few basic things about his business, such as 1) who in their right mind would choose to do this work? 2) who would agree to get paid so little to do it? and 3) where did people think a job like this would ever lead?

John started to view his team members a little differently after that. As he explained, "I realized that we were playing a losing game by focusing on how we could get the most of our people while paying them as little as we could get away with. How could we expect great performance and expect cultural buy-in by thinking that way?" Instead he started to ask himself: "What kinds of things can we do to give that mopping more meaning?"

That's when he says they really started focusing on people as their main strategy, and not just because of "all the humanitarian positives" but because he believed it would "build a stronger business."

That mindset shift made him start looking at how to run his business in a new way, and that led to a bunch of new actions. They started offering things to employees that would really make a difference in their lives, such as transportation discounts and English classes for employees who didn't speak English as their first language, which allowed them to "give better service in our restaurants, but also gave them a chance to move onto better jobs, even ones outside the company." They also created comfortable lounge areas where employees could take their breaks, instead of sitting in the dining room, checking their texts while there was a line of customers out the door. As far as wages were concerned, they aimed to build a business model where they could hire the best and pay accordingly. As an example, in 2001 they increased the minimum pay for every person in the company to $8 an hour, even though minimum wage at the time was only $5.15 an hour.

John acknowledges that raising wages was a risky move, but he also believes it paid off. The next year and in the years that followed, they saw record sales and profits and the business continued to grow.

John believes that one of the key reasons these changes were successful is because he involved employees in the process. He describes "sitting there with people in a room and having long discussions and debates about their futures and what we were going to do for them." He and other leaders in the company said, "We're going to do this or do that, because you've told us it matters, but it's not just a gift. We're making a deal with each of you that you'll help the business earn these new benefits. We're paying you an advance on this handshake deal, because we trust you." Today John says that making those changes were among the most important and impactful things he ever did at Boloco, all because that one late night, when he mopped the floor, allowed him to start seeing things differently.

## Action Items

- Make sure your organization has a purpose statement that inspires people. Answer the *why* for your company.
- Communicate it clearly and often so everyone in the organization gets the picture. Use technology to reinforce it.
- Understand the mission, vision and values of your company and help your employees understand them as well.
- Work on becoming an authentic, self-aware leader who engages in behaviors that make people feel you believe they matter. Be open, curious and vulnerable as a leader with your team.

# CHAPTER 4

# The Science behind
# the Art of Hiring

ONE OF THE THINGS we talked about in Chapter 1 was that engagement begins even before a person is hired. It begins with the first point of contact, when someone applies for a job with your company. The application and hiring process is so important because it sets the tone for the relationship between employer and employee. It's also important because, in this new economy, companies need more than ever to have the right people on their teams. The wrong people can damage a brand when they are on the job, and they cost time, money and energy when they leave and have to be replaced—and all that trouble just because they weren't a good fit to begin with.

A lot of employers think that hiring is a matter of resume and chemistry, but there are many more tools that employers can use today for a quicker and more effective process. At PeopleMatter, we knew from the start that assessments were going to be a very important part of not only the hiring process but also the ongoing development process of employees, which is why we have built them into our software. They remove much of the guesswork so you don't have to rely solely on your gut.

That's not to say that your gut instinct isn't important. I believe there's a lot of merit in relying on your gut for a hiring decision or a potential promotion, but that should be just one part of the process. Assessments provide another dimension, an objective way to look at an individual and uncover certain motivators or drivers that you might not have known about otherwise. Assessments can even help the employer better engage people by providing some context for how the employee likes to be engaged.

## FINDINGS FROM PMI'S *HOW HOURLY WORKFORCES WORK* SURVEY

- More than two out of three service-industry businesses don't find it easy to identify high-quality candidates.

- Ten thousand dollars: Cost to replace a manager for one out of five businesses.

- One out of five managers spends more than five hours each week completing hiring-related tasks.

- Managers using multiple hiring systems are 2.5 times more likely to spend 10+ hours a week on hiring-related tasks, compared to those using a workforce management system.

Back in 2011 PeopleMatter started a relationship with People-Clues, which is a global provider of assessment technology for employee screening, selection and development. At first, we partnered with PeopleClues and then ended up acquiring the company, and it has been one of the most fantastic acquisitions we have ever made. I have gained a tremendous wealth of information on the science behind the art of hiring because of our work with Julie Moreland, who is Senior Vice President of PeopleClues. She has dedicated her entire career to coming up with ways to ensure that a candidate or employee is a good fit for a position.

The following is what I have learned from Julie in her own words:

## Julie Moreland on the Science behind Hiring

We've made the bold statement that people matter in this book. At the end of the day, if that's what we stand for, then we want to do everything we can to make sure that we put our people in a position to be successful, one where they can grow and contribute to the organization.

The number-one reason why people fail at their jobs—why they are not able to contribute, why they leave or get fired—is a lack of job fit. And even though we've done all of these things to get them into the organization and then train them, the number-one reason why that doesn't work is that they didn't fit the job to begin with. So there are two losers when this happens: the organization certainly loses the talent and the time, money and energy that has gone into those employees, and then those individuals lose their job, their time and their effort, and they are going to take that failure with them.

Instead, we want to do everything we can to make sure we are setting people up for success from the first day they are brought into the organization.

A couple of analogies here: If we were going to invest in a

company, would we invest in it based solely on our gut? I hope not. We would look at the P&Ls and balance sheets. We would interview executives in that organization. We would look at the track record. Then we might rely on our gut to help us make a final decision. We should be doing the same thing with this valuable asset that we're bringing in and that we're going to spend a lot of money on over time—our people.

Like Nate, I believe that the gut is incredibly important, but we want to have some information that we can rely on first, before we turn the decision over to our gut. The best thing we can do is arm hiring managers with behavioral information that will help them make their own judgment calls. Give them information about people to determine if those people have what I call the "raw material" to be a good fit for the position. Raw material is information about whether a candidate's core behavioral traits match what you're looking for in a certain position. And if they do, then you interview that person and let your gut take over to see if you feel that candidate is going to be the right person for your team or for a particular store location. That's the beauty of bringing your gut together with objective job fit information: you know before you even meet the person that she already has the raw material to be successful in that position.

We collect that raw material by assessing everybody the same way and getting core measurements that are stable. Around the globe, psychologists universally agree that there are five things you can measure reliably. Then, you can compare the results of those measurements to the job you need to fill. These core measurements are called the Big Five.

We measure the Big Five traits for every person in the same way, just as a tailor or a seamstress would use a standard measuring tape to make any kind of garment. The five things fit the acronym CLUES. We are measuring people clues, and we want to take those clues and use them to match people to different jobs and cultures.

## THE FIVE CLUES

**C stands for conscientiousness.** This is about whether someone is well organized and detail oriented. Some jobs need more detail-oriented people than other jobs do. We put that measurement on a normative bell curve. Compared to the population, you fall either on the left-hand side of the curve, which is not very detail oriented; the right-hand side, which very detail oriented; or the fat part of the bell curve in the middle, which is average. There is no bad place to be on the bell curve, but knowing where you are allows us to compare you to the job we are filling to see if you have the level of detail orientation that is needed. In other words, we're answering, "Are you a good or bad fit?"

**L stands for likeability.** Somebody who rates high on the scale of likeability is someone who wants to be liked and wants to please people. The opposite end of that bell curve is someone who is very tough-minded, skeptical, direct and determined. In the service industry, most roles require a person to be on the high likability side of the bell curve. But the minute we get into management roles, where people have to deal with disciplinary issues, traits such as directness and determination are, typically, more important.

**U stands for unconventionality.** These are people who are very unconventional and flexible in their thinking. They change and like to be creative in the way they approach things. The other side of that bell curve is people who are conventional and rules based. This is an important one in the service industry because of safety. People who tend to be highly flexible think, "Well, maybe I don't need to pick up that mop and move it out of somebody's way to keep them from falling." They don't necessarily follow the rules. But they can be very creative, which is useful in other sorts of situations. Again, it just depends upon what the job needs them to be.

**E stands for extraversion.** This is probably one of the more obvious ones. Is the applicant an outspoken, highly energetic, very extraverted person? Or is the applicant more of an introverted listener and more cautious in terms of risk taking? In the service industry, this one can have a big influence on whether someone fits better in front of house or back of house. In front of house, you've got to have that warm, friendly, extraverted personality. But in back of house, you actually want people to be a little bit more reserved because they are not having as much interaction with the customer.

**S stands for stability.** This is about whether or not somebody tends to handle stress well or, in other words, has stress resistance. On the other end of the scale is someone who tends to be more emotional and sensitive and, therefore, less stable. Some positions require a little higher level of stability than do others.

## USING THE DATA

The examples I have given pertain to the service industry, but this works universally, for any business. PeopleClues works with organizations in eight countries, using multiple languages, and spanning many industries, including automobile sales, health care and technology.

We measure people and then we use those measurements for multiple purposes. We use them to narrow down a list of candidates so you don't have to interview every single person to find the best one. Then, we use them to provide behavioral interview questions that you can ask to dive deeper with those individuals who have the right raw material. We do that so employers and managers don't have to think about what they should be asking Joe versus Mary versus Sally but, instead, can focus on exactly what they need to know about each person. The questions are built around not only where the person fell on those bell curves on the assessment but also the type of job you are asking them to do. We call them smart questions, because now this hiring manager, who knows nothing about this person and may not have been trained all that well on how to interview or hire people, is asking really smart questions that will get him the answers he needs.

We use the data not only to decide whom to hire but for onboarding as well. Say you have a supervisor who is getting a new employee named Joe, and she doesn't know Joe. The onboarding report will give that supervisor some tips about what motivates Joe and how to get him up to speed more quickly.

Then, let's say we bring Joe in, and he does a really good job and is interested in moving up. Of course, people matter, so we want to grow them. We can look into that data and see if Joe might have the characteristics to go into leadership. Maybe Joe isn't perfect for leadership, based on his assessment, but the assessment helps us understand what development he needs, so we can then provide tips to help him build those skills.

Behavioral scores rarely change much. It is sort of like being baked. Between the ages of 6 and 12, your core traits are pretty well done, and they don't move much after that. But we can build skills to help enhance a person's level of competency for performing certain types of jobs, which leads to greater satisfaction and engagement. We can also work around a person's weaker areas if we know what they are. If you are missing an ingredient for a particular job, you can still be very effective at that job if you are aware of the issue and you work on it.

"Live hospitality" is part of our core values at PeopleMatter and an important component of our hiring process. We use our own assessment tests to find right-fit applicants who share this passion.

The problem comes when an employee has two or three traits that don't fit the job. Now that person is spending so much energy trying to be the way the job needs him to be that he isn't actually bringing much of his energy to "doing" the job. This leads to frustration and lack of engagement.

Over the years, we have developed benchmarks for more than 125 common jobs. We also encourage clients to do custom benchmarking studies. That is where we figure out what works in their specific environments. Many companies will have a unique aspect to their culture and the way they have designed their jobs. A cashier is a cashier in some respects, but some organizations might say, "Well, we want our cashiers to upsell," which means the cashier will need certain personality traits that are a little different from the cashier who is just taking people's money. Our general categories are a bit broad because they have to accommodate a cashier in different types of environments. The way to get the best value out of the measurements is to actually go through a custom benchmarking study so we can distinctly define what you are looking for in your company.

## DOMINO FOOD AND FUEL

"Our stores have different dynamics; some have more truck drivers as customers while other locations have become more like a neighborhood store, with regulars who stop in for coffee and the latest news. The applicants bring their own strengths. People can be the right fit for different locations. We can use [PeopleMatter's] pre-screening assessments, filtering capabilities and ability to review all applications at the corporate level to staff each location with candidates who are the best fit. Our store managers are really loving it."

**–Amy Smith, Vice President, Domino Food and Fuel**

### WHEN YOU DON'T HAVE DATA

Employers and managers who rely solely on their gut tend to hire people who are similar to themselves. When they conduct interviews, they are not really thinking about whether this person is going to be good for that job. They are thinking, "Did I like her?" or "Did I have a good feeling about him?" Those things are important, but you should have some objective data to verify what you thought you saw. Plus, hiring people like you can mean you end up with a team of people with similar strengths and similar weaknesses rather than complementary ones.

## MISUSING THE DATA

"We had a convenience store chain that was using PeopleMatter for their hiring processes, and they saw a tenfold increase in the number of applicants they received. It overwhelmed their managers, so instead of following good hiring practices, they looked at the assessment results and just picked the first names that popped up in green. But green just indicates that the applicant has the basic raw material the company is looking for and that the system suggests they move forward in the process. That was a disaster for them because they were not using the tool correctly. It actually negatively impacted their turnover. But we were able to work with them to turn the situation around."

**–Mark Deaton, former Senior Vice President of Customer Care, PeopleMatter**

One of the biggest complaints I hear is that companies are really struggling with managers. This happens because people perform really well and are interested in management, so they get promoted. But they haven't been assessed for a leadership position and their scores haven't been compared to those of successful leaders. To make matters worse, the sad reality is that most companies don't provide any leadership training. So, high-performing people get promoted into management jobs, but they don't possess the raw material for job fit and haven't been trained on leader skill sets. You need a different skill set to be a manager. You need to know how to hold effective meetings, how to delegate tasks, and how to give constructive feedback. This is an engagement disaster for the team that person manages, because those employees are not getting what they need from their manager. Remember that phrase, "People leave managers, not companies"? The two key drivers for turnover and disengagement are bad job fit and poor management.

## THE BENEFITS OF DATA

Using assessments not only helps you be more effective in deciding whom to hire, it can also streamline your processes and save you time. Let's say you have 25 people who have applied for a position. The assessments tell you which five people you should focus your time on, because they have the raw material you need. Then, instead of sifting through 25 candidates and interviewing all of them, you only have to sit down with five. This lets you spend your precious time, which isn't scalable—time is the only thing that we can't scale—with only those people who have the raw material.

Hiring the right people also saves you time later on. So many managers focus their time and energy on helping struggling employees and trying to get them to improve their weak areas or deficiencies. If you think about it, this doesn't make sense, because while you are focusing on trying to fix certain employees, you are not developing the good performers to make them even better, which is really a better use of your time. But if you hire the right people, then you can focus your development time on their strengths and help them improve their contributions to the company, which in turn drives engagement.

In Chapter One we talked about the three important things Gallup suggested companies do to raise engagement levels, which are 1) hire the right people, 2) develop their strengths, and 3) invest in their well-being. Hiring for fit by using a combination of assessments and instinct will surely help you improve your track record for the first suggestion, but it will also give you precious time to dedicate to points two and three. If you step back and take an honest look at where your management time is going and discover that it's mostly spent fixing problems or dealing with struggling employees, then you are not going to have the time you need to develop good employees and invest in their well-being.

## ROADRUNNER MARKETS

"We started our relationship with PeopleMatter in 2010. We wanted to use their hiring platform because we just didn't feel like we were getting the right kind of applicants that we needed to fill our positions. We were, more or less, just getting warm bodies and not the type of people we were looking for. We really wanted to find people with the values we were looking for, with the attitude we were looking for, such as loyalty, honesty, and a service mentality of wanting to help others. We wanted to hire people who had the right character rather than just people who were the right age and had a vehicle they could use to get to work. PeopleMatter was exactly what we were looking for."

**–Ryan Broyles, President and CEO, Roadrunner Markets**

Another benefit of a hiring platform like ours is everything is automated and fast. It's instant; there's no wait time. When the economic downturn happened, millions of people in this country were abused. They were desperate to get a job, so they went out and filled out long applications at numerous places. They took test after test. They did all this, and, most of the time, they never heard anything back. Not a thing. They didn't even know if their materials had been seen. If we agree that people matter, then treating them poorly in the application process is abuse. But a system like ours makes it easy to not only assure applicants that you've received their materials, but also to give them information on their personality traits. We can provide them meaningful insight about their strengths and how to better present those strengths in their résumés and interviews. We do that just because they applied for the job and filled out an assessment. In that way, we are helping these people, regardless of whether we hire them, because we believe they matter. And they get that from the company when most other companies aren't even letting applicants know the company received their application. Doing this lets them have a positive experience, a positive impression of the company's brand, even if they don't get the job.

If you think about it, in the service industry, the people who are applying for your jobs are also your customers. That's why it's so important to provide them with a positive experience. And if they don't have one, they are probably going to post something on Facebook or Twitter that says, "Whatever you do, don't waste your time interviewing at this place. It was a long process, it was no fun, and they never even responded to me." Things like that can be very damaging to a brand in the service industry.

## Customer Story: Fiesta Mart

Fiesta Mart is an international supermarket chain based in Houston, Texas, and is a prime example of how having the right hiring processes in place pays off.

Since many of the company's employment applicants speak Spanish as their primary language, it was important to Fiesta to be able to offer hiring assessments in Spanish. PeopleMatter was able to accommodate that request, and Spanish-speaking applicants found that being able to go through the application process in their native language made for a more positive experience.

Fiesta Mart has used PeopleMatter to open three new stores. One store is smaller, with only 100 employees, but approximately 200 people were hired for each of the two other stores. Every single person hired for all three stores went through the PeopleMatter Platform. According to their director of human resources, Wanda Parish, "Hiring at those stores was the easiest experience the company has ever had. Plus, the employees hired through PeopleMatter tend to be more computer-savvy and adapt easily to the learning environment we are developing in partnership with PeopleMatter. It's a well known maxim that well-trained employees are happier, perform better and tend to stay longer."

Fiesta says it now wouldn't hire any other way. As Wanda put it, "The traits measured by PeopleClues assessments parallel Fiesta's culture very closely, so an added bonus for us is that we have insight into which applicants have the best chance of fitting into our organization."

## Action Items

The following action items are from Julie Moreland's book *Women Who Mean Business*. In it, she makes four simple recommendations to companies looking to improve their hiring practices:

- **Define the job concisely with quantifiable terms (and review every year):**
  a. Define "success" by looking at current employees. How do you know if they are being successful? Something has to be measured and defined.
  b. Use a valid behavioral assessment to create a benchmark for success that shows a proven track record of what behavioral competencies work in your environment, management style and in the specific job.
  c. Define the KSAs (knowledge, skills, abilities). What skill sets and experiences have proven to be the most successful in this position?
  d. Replace generalities such as "must be a team player" with specifics such as "must continually collaborate with a five-person team and maintain an 80 percent or higher customer-satisfaction rating."

- **Make sure your screening process covers three key areas in terms of fit:** attitude and level of engagement, skills and experience and behavioral competency. Most processes only cover one or two of these. (Note: when hiring for entry-level jobs, most of your candidates are right out of school and don't have experience yet, so you *have to* make sure you at least have the other two components to make good decisions.)

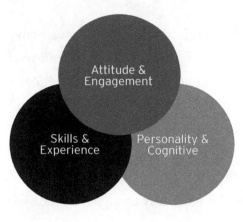

**1. Attitude & Engagement
(Company Fit)**
What are the individual's attitudes toward work and work-related issues? Using assessments, behavioral interviews and 360-degree surveys, measure counter-productive behaviors that might affect his/her ability to be a productive employee.

**2. Personality & Cognitive
(Job Fit & Development)**
What are the individual's personality characteristics and cognitive abilities? Using assessments and behavioral interviews, measure job fit and determine areas for coaching, development and leadership.

**3. Skills & Experience (Job Fit & Development)**
What level of skills does the individual have for various job-related tasks? Using demonstrations and skills tests, assess his/her level of skill for particular job-related tasks.

- **Think of candidates as customers.** How much does your company spend to get "eyeballs" on your company, product or service? Imagine your candidates are your potential customers, who, in turn, will help you make sure your process provides a good candidate experience. This is a marketing opportunity that most companies totally miss. Your process should be automated as much as possible and it should let candidates know where they are in the process and do something to help them in their career search. Provide tips, even coupons for your products/services and anything you can in your process to help them. You can actually provide them automated feedback on job fit, or lack thereof, which is the greatest gift you can give people for truly finding the right job in the future.

- **Make sure your screening process is efficient.** Every minute spent by your staff is precious and not scalable! Utilize technology to educate prospective employees, gather and organize information, and communicate with those prospective employees about where they stand in your process. Spend your "labor" time of precious minutes with individuals who rise to the top of the heap and who have the best overall fit and then choose between those using your behavioral interviews. Remember to keep this technology *simple*. There are lots of choices in the market for applicant tracking, assessments and background check services. Look for easy and efficient tools for your hiring managers to use.

## SCOTTY'S BREWHOUSE

"To guarantee the best service, we have an intense onboarding and training program for new hires. One of the things I've observed with PeopleMatter is that we're seeing far fewer new hires drop out, because we're able to focus our hiring process on stronger candidates."

**–Scott Wise, Founder and CEO, Scotty's Brewhouse**

## CASE STUDY: APPLE SAUCE

Manual tracking, screening and onboarding methods produced disjointed hiring practices for Apple Sauce, Inc., a major franchisee of Applebee's Neighborhood Bar and Grill. New hires were spending three-fifths of their onboarding time filling out paperwork, and processing paperwork manually took up company time and resources, plus it led to data mistakes, which meant more time spent following up on missing employee information.

PeopleMatter provided the company with a cloud-based platform that allowed the company to connect all its human resource processes within six weeks. We also provided the company with seamless integration into its social media outlets, which enabled the company to proactively recruit mobile-social, tech-savvy talent.

### Return on Investment

- The company improved the overall quality of its applicant pool.

- It saved its hiring managers, on average, 244 hours per month.

- It reduced onboarding paperwork by 92 percent.

- It improved employee engagement and retention rates.

### Customer Reaction

"The thing I've liked most about PeopleMatter is our ability to integrate it into all our social media outlets. We've built out this huge pool of resources."
**–Bruce Dodge, Regional Human Resource Director**

..................................

# CASE STUDY: ST. JOE PETROLEUM

St. Joe Petroleum is a family-owned business that is based in St. Joseph, Missouri, and operates eight Fastgas convenience stores. The company's paper-based applications and HR data were decentralized by unit, so PeopleMatter provided a platform solution that centralized all the information, automated the application process and simplified schedule creation and distribution.

### Return on Investment

- St. Joe saw a 50 percent increase in applications, an improvement in new hire quality and a reduction in turnover of 24 percent.

- The company saved $49,500 in annual tax credits.

- Managers could create employee schedules 67 percent faster and post employee notifications eight days sooner.

- The company saw a reduction in overtime of 13 percent.

### Customer Reaction

"PeopleMatter is a great thing for employee morale. We've actually given them the power to do what we ask them to do."
**–Matt Flynn, Director of Retail Operations**

# CHAPTER 5

# Engage People in a New Way

**WHEN I THINK ABOUT ENGAGING EMPLOYEES** today, I think about two things. The first is technology, or more specifically, using technology as a communication channel. Technology, in and of itself, is not going to solve anyone's engagement problem, but it can be a valuable tool that enables you to communicate with your workforce on a regular basis.

The other thing I think about is the personal or human interaction that you have with people—the tone, the tenor, and the timing of how you communicate with them. This can mean things such as what we do at PeopleMatter in our weekly patio meetings and quarterly town hall meetings. It can mean something as simple as the power of a handwritten note, which is a personal touch one of the founders of MAD Greens, Marley Hodgson, uses to welcome new team members. Every company uses different channels and different communication styles to engage people. The point is to find what works for you and for the culture of your company.

In Part I of this book we talked about how, in today's market, old ways of communicating with and engaging people just don't work as well as they used to. The old way was a "command and control" structure, in which people were often viewed as human doings rather than human beings. We've already talked about how defining guiding forces such as your purpose, your mission and your values can help you create a culture in which people are seen as whole beings. That and hiring for fit are the first steps in engaging people. But there is more that can be done to invest in our employees' development and well-being.

## Tool: The Four Ps

Leadership coach and team-building expert Mark Tribus says, "There are four things that describe great leaders these days, which I call the Four Ps." Great leaders are

1. professional;
2. passionate about what they do;
3. personal in their approach—they see the individual, not just the team or organization;
4. persistent in their own development and the development of others.

## Feedback

Traditional performance reviews suck, especially as a way of engaging people. Why do they suck? Because they often don't look at the right aspects of the individual, they are very one-sided, and they don't fit today's culture and workforce. But that doesn't mean feedback isn't important. In fact, the PeopleMatter Institute's 2013 *How Hourly Workforces Work* survey found that businesses that regularly and consistently provide performance feedback are two times less likely to report turnover greater than 100 percent than are those that provide feedback annually or inconsistently. Companies that don't evaluate hourly employees' performance at all are three times more likely to report turnover greater than 100 percent. Feedback is clearly important, but there are more engaging ways to provide it than your typical annual or quarterly review with a manager.

## FREQUENT INFORMAL FEEDBACK

As we discussed in Chapter 2, millennials want to be engaged through technology, which is a major way they communicate in the rest of their lives. And there is another advantage to using technology: it allows employers to give feedback in real time. There is a new theory known as frequent informal feedback, or FIF as it's often called, which describes a more effective way of interacting with employees. It's also the kind of feedback we like to give team members at PeopleMatter. It's frequent, which means people don't have to wait for the annual or quarterly performance review to roll around to get some information about how they're doing, and it's informal, because it's not a structured document in which you have to fill out Parts A, B, C, and D. Instead, generally, it's technology driven, operating similarly to the way in which Yelp operates by giving individuals the opportunity to rate and comment on their experiences with coworkers, employees and even management. It allows people to have a real-time performance evaluation that is transparent.

The service industry lends itself very well to this type of feedback. Lots of companies today are giving customers the opportunity to provide feedback on their experiences. Another benefit of frequent informal feedback is that when it comes time for a more formal performance review, data is already present to provide a reality check on a manager's opinion about an employee. If the customers are raving about the service of a certain employee, then the employer can take that into account, even if that employer hasn't personally witnessed those interactions.

## 4DX

4DX stands for the four disciplines of execution, which are 1) focus on the wildly important, 2) act on the lead measures, 3) keep a compelling scoreboard, and 4) create a cadence of accountability. This is a tool that was put together by Franklin Covey (there's also a book titled *The 4 Disciplines of Execution: Achieving Your Wildly Important Goals* by Chris McChesney, Jim Huling and bestselling author Sean Covey), and it was designed to drive engagement at every level of an organization.

You start by setting one or two wildly important goals (WIGs) that you want the company to accomplish. Then you develop your lead and lag measures, which tell you how you're going to be able influence those wildly important goals. Next, you develop a scoreboard that, basically, tells you if you're winning or not. And, finally, you set up a system of accountability, in which all those involved meet once a week to talk about what they did that week and to make commitments about how they are going to continue to influence those lead measures.

I like to use the example of losing weight to help put 4DX in perspective. Let's say you want to lose 25 pounds. That's your wildly important goal, your WIG. But that's a pretty big goal, so you focus on more specific, incremental things that will help you get there. You decide you need to exercise 30 minutes each day and limit your daily calorie intake to 1,200. Those are your lead measures. Your lag measure is the number on the scale. That tells you how well you're doing and if your lead measures are effective. To help keep you on track, you join a support group—companies such as Jenny Craig and Weight Watchers have weekly meetings and online forums to help hold members accountable—at which you talk about what you did last week and what you're going to do next week.

Hitting our 1-millionth applicant was a huge priority for our entire company early on ... and a huge celebration once we did!

4DX is a great tool for getting everyone focused on top priorities and continually driving toward them. We adopted this methodology at PeopleMatter and then built our own scoreboard technology to be able to track whether or not we were executing it. Every single department throughout the company creates a bulletin board or a chart or something that is fairly visible so that when people walk by, they can easily see, with just a glance, what that team is going after and if it is meeting its goals. Those charts are updated on a weekly basis.

The purpose behind this methodology is to streamline what you're doing, so you aren't focused so much on what Franklin Covey calls the "whirlwind" of activity or the day-to-day e-mails, phone calls, crises and other distractions that pop up every day in your life. You set your focus firmly on establishing achievable goals, working toward them, and sharing your progress with the rest of the company. Often, individuals can't see how their job contributes to the company as a whole. 4DX forces the organization to dig deep for every position and tie performance back to its WIGs. Individuals who can see how they're contributing by literally looking at a scoreboard are highly engaged to do the activities that they cocreated and bought into.

## Gamification

The rise of gamification is something we're seeing a lot in various industries. It has been around from a personal-use standpoint for a while now, but it's moving into the workplace as a tool for engaging people. Gamification in this context is the concept of using games to drive behavior and outcomes. Do you remember Foursquare? In that game, the user who checked in most often became mayor of that particular location. This same sort of concept—where users aspire to get more points so they can choose some type of reward—is being put into practice in the workplace for training and behavior incentives. For example, the store that sells the most of something during a certain period in the day can earn points that are redeemable for a paid day off or maybe a small bonus, some kind of reward that the employer decides is going to be meaningful to employees. Employers can use these kinds of games to drive the behaviors and outcomes they want.

We have been working with Thorntons convenience store chain on using the ideas behind gamification to help the company reach its BHAG, or big hairy audacious goal (a term from Jim Collins and Jerry Porras's book *Built to Last*) of selling 1,000 cups of coffee or soft drinks a day in each of its stores. It's a really big goal, but the company has hit that goal in many of its stores, so it's not impossible to do. The potential outcome for the company is huge if that goal is hit in *all* the stores. If the company can sell that many drinks, it is going to create more customer traffic and increase sales, because customers are going to buy other things such as a magazine or newspaper, a bag of chips, some gum, or they may make some other impulsive purchase that strikes them while they're paying for that cup of coffee or soda. That's the downstream effect of getting people into stores to buy those drinks. It builds frequent, repeat business, and it encourages people, hopefully, to buy other products that they see once they are inside the store.

For our part, we can setup a game on our platform that rewards the first store that gets to 1,000 cups with a paid day off or some other benefit. We can create a real-time game with a leader board, on which everyone can see and track the number of cups being sold at each location and the number of points each store is racking up as a result, creating some friendly competition among stores and motivating employees as a result.

## Rewards and Recognition

I believe people want to be appreciated for their work. It's amazing to watch how being recognized publicly for great work affects people. You can see it on their faces when they're praised in front of their peers. Recognition of this kind can have just as much of a meaningful impact on a person as a raise would have. People will work even harder for you because they feel so appreciated.

A little praise—and more cowbell!—can go a long way toward making team members feel engaged and respected.

The management team at PeopleMatter came up with the concept of shout-outs to use internally to recognize our team members for a job well done. We give shout-outs to people through technology, and we also do them in person, during our weekly patio meetings. We have a standard format for the content we cover at every patio meeting. The first thing we cover is introductions of new team members or promotions that are notable. Then we have a quick two-minute update from each department. Finally, we talk about shout-outs from the senior management team.

We come up with our weekly shout-outs from the senior management team meetings that are held every Monday afternoon, and in those meetings, everybody brings in the name of one person who exemplified one of our core values during the prior week. We go around the table and each senior manager has one minute to mention someone's name, describe what that person did, and explain which value that person exemplified. It's a way to highlight all the good things our team members are working so hard to achieve. We have 10 senior managers, so this only takes about 10 minutes. Then we write down the names of the people being recognized and we swap so senior managers get the name of someone they don't usually work with. For example, the CFO might get the name of a person who is being recognized from the marketing team, or the head of sales will get the name of an engineer. Then it's up to each manager to thank that person working in another department. My two requirements are that it cannot be done via e-mail—it must be done in person or by phone—and it must be done within 24 hours of the management meeting so the person is recognized "in the moment." The senior manager will say something like, "Hey, I was in a management meeting this week, and the head of your department mentioned your name and said you'd been working really hard. You have gone above and beyond for us, and I just want to thank you for all your hard work. You are really exemplifying our value of 'teamwork.'"

I believe this is a great way of making people feel appreciated and also of creating interactions within the organization between people who would normally never be in contact with one another. And we don't stop there. We also pick two people from the group we are recognizing—because we can't do all 10—and announce them in front of the whole company at that week's patio meeting held on Tuesdays. Then, we end each patio meeting with our company cheer. Everyone claps when we're done, and that ends the meeting in a really positive way.

## Communication Style and Personal Touches

Human interactions, whether in person or through some sort of technology platform, are an equally important part of engaging people.

Treating employees like customers is a popular concept in human resource management today, and that includes how you communicate with them.

The former Human Resource Director at Souper Salad, Vivien Horton, told us a story that we thought was totally cool. She decided to incorporate some of what she was teaching her employees about communicating with customers into her own communication style. For example, she was teaching her employees about effectively setting up and managing expectations for the customer, which Mark Deaton, our Senior Vice President Of Customer Care at the time, describes as "one of the core tenets of best-of-class service." He continues, "Many companies allow open-ended expectations (I'll get back to you soon.), and they don't empower their support teams to take ownership of a problem ("I'll open a ticket for you ... here's the number ... check back later"). A more effective communication technique is to set clear expectations ("I'll get back to you no later than end of business on Wednesday"), and then hold people accountable for meeting or exceeding them."

Vivien took this idea and decided to incorporate it into her own communication approach with her store managers. And they were very appreciative of the effort. After she did this, she got several spontaneous e-mails and phone calls over the course of a couple months from managers who wanted to thank her for being such a great communicator.

Taking time out of my day to ask people how they're doing—and really listen to the answer—or to call and check in are some of the simple things I like to do to connect with people on my team and show them that I care about them. I also like to find small ways to show my appreciation to the partners and spouses of our team members. I do this by handwriting cards for them or sending them gift baskets. Sometimes, I will give team members a gift certificate to take their significant other out to dinner. At big company events I try to make sure I thank this group of people, because I think their contributions to our success are often overlooked. They are the people who support our people and allow us all to do what we do each and every day. And if they didn't, we wouldn't be as successful as we are.

We do similar things in our customer experience department to make our own customers feel valued. We once sent flowers to a client whose pet had just died or sometimes we'll make personal visits to local clients instead of calling or e-mailing them. These are ways that we can exceed their expectations. Whether the gesture is aimed at an employee or a customer, it's the same idea. Even small things—a simple e-mail, a spoken word, a note, an apology, or a gift—can have a real impact on people and make them feel valued. That's why they are an important part of our personal communication style at PeopleMatter.

You have to develop your own communication style that is going to work for you and your business, one that you are comfortable with, that fits your culture, and that you are going to be able to consistently maintain. Consistency is key because it shows people that they are truly important to you, which is why our patio meetings take place every week without fail, no matter what's going on in the business.

Personal communication doesn't have to be in person, either. Technology can be a great tool to use to maintain that consistency. In building our technology, we have always strived to find ways to empower organizations to better communicate with their workforces, and vice-versa. Technology can also be a great communication tool for large companies or ones that maintain multiple offices. Let's face it. If a company has 6,000 employees, the CEO is not going to be able to have face-to-face contact with everybody. But what he can do is have contact through technology, which allows him to engage with those people on a frequent basis and still have a personal connection.

For our new building's grand opening, we shut down King Street and threw a party to celebrate our new headquarters, our success, and all of the people and customers who helped us get there.

## ENGAGING CUSTOMERS

Twice a year at PeopleMatter, we send team members out on what we call our Listening Matters Tour, where they visit with our customers all across the country. Everyone from executives to developers pair up to meet face-to-face with PeopleMatter users and listen to what's working for them, what's not, what they like, and what they need. We'll also help them through any issues they're having and show them new platform features that are coming out next.

On one of our Listening Matters tours, we visited Fiesta Mart, which is headquartered in Houston, Texas. He happened to be there for the opening day of the grocery chain's 63rd store. Wanda Parish, Director of HR for Fiesta Mart and a huge PeopleMatter fan, told us how incredibly thankful she and her entire team were for PeopleMatter and the big role our hiring software had played in the opening of that store. She said they used PeopleMatter to hire every single person at the new store—all 200-plus team members, from the general manager all the way down. Wanda said that companywide, Fiesta Mart was hiring better people and that their turnover rate was lower. I loved this story, because it serves as a huge testament to the value PeopleMatter brings to the Fiesta Mart team.

## Tool: 7-45-48

Louis Basile of Wildflower Bread Company feels it's important to build a culture in which people feel safe enough to be who they are and express their opinions. His company uses a communication tool set called Safe Space® that was created by Miick and Associates. As Louis explains, "We spend a lot of time talking about Safe Space and the respectful way that you have conversations with folks, how you can not only share your perspective on a particular issue or subject, but also be an incredibly good listener so that you can let other people share their perspectives too."

One of the tools in the set is called 7-45-48 and it reminds you that when you are developing your own communication style, you need to consider more than words.

When translating what we say and do, the people with whom we interact take meaning or translate meaning in the following way:

- **seven** percent of people take meaning from words spoken;
- **forty-five** percent take meaning from body language—there are 3,000 facial expressions that mean exactly the same thing, globally;
- **forty-eight** percent take meaning from tone of voice.

This means that:

    a. body language and tone make up 93 percent of the translation;

    b. if I want to ensure my effectiveness in communication, I had better work to have my tone of voice and body language match my words;

    c. there is a paradox in that:

        i. my word choice is very important, not less important;

        ii. words mean less when body language and tone don't match the words.

**Cautions to take note of:**

- Pay attention to sarcasm. It's funny until it's not. It's clear but not.
- Be kind and courageous enough to actually speak the truth instead of "hiding behind" sarcasm.
- Watch out for pronouns (he, she, it, they). Instead make "I" statements in SafeSpace.

At PeopleMatter, we're serious about providing awesome service—serious enough to deck out an RV and take it on a nationwide tour, just to make sure our customers are happy.

## The Payoff of Engagement

The payoff of having more engaged employees should be obvious by now. To give one more example, at PeopleMatter we provide learning modules that are video based to train team members at restaurants or stores. Think about how much more engaging and effective it can be to learn how the company wants you to make its burritos from watching a video on your phone rather than reading an old-fashioned, paper manual. And if it's more engaging, people are more likely to pay close attention. They will learn better and faster. That will have an effect on the quality of food they prepare, which, in turn, will have an effect on customer satisfaction. And higher customer satisfaction leads to higher sales, more repeat business, positive word of mouth, and so on. The payoff, in other words, can be huge. (More on these kinds of "downstream effects" in the next chapter.)

In the service businesses we work with, the effect that more engaged employees can have on the business is often obvious from the moment you walk in the door. Ryan Broyles, President and CEO of Roadrunner Markets, a family-owned convenience store chain started by his father and operating in 92 locations across four states, says he has witnessed this in his own stores. Twice a year, he and his management team go out on what they call "pride rides," which are tours of their stores, during which they perform a 136-point inspection. Individual stores receive awards for getting the highest scores in various categories, such as the cleanest restroom. (One year, the award for that category was a gold plunger!) Ryan explains, "The stores get graded during our pride rides, but it's really more about giving our employees a chance to show their pride in their stores."

## ON COMMUNICATING WITH EMPLOYEES

"We had an employee who fell and broke his back. So that he could go on leave, I helped out by managing his shifts. PeopleMatter SCHEDULE™ made communicating the situation to my team easier. I put messages in, explaining what happened and asking for back up. People were really responsive to that."

**–Betsy Miller, Director of Human Resources and Operations, Franklin Restaurant Group**

Roadrunner Markets has been doing its pride rides for a number of years, but ever since it went through what Ryan describes as a "cultural revolution" a few years back, where it refocused on why it was in business and why employees would want to show up to work every day, he says he can really "see the difference on employees' faces" when he goes on these rides. They are clearly proud of their stores and happy to be there, and if they get maybe a not-so-great score on their inspection, he says, "They take it seriously. Some folks get pretty emotional and pretty upset about it. It's the same with those who receive the highest scores. They get overwhelmed in the moment and some even break into tears."

## FINDINGS FROM PMI'S *HOW HOURLY WORKFORCES WORK* SURVEY

- Forty-three percent of businesses are not satisfied with the frequency of performance reviews at their organization.

- Forty-one percent of businesses do not have a full understanding of why employees leave.

- Three out of five businesses don't find it easy to record and track hourly employee performance.

- Identifying and nurturing future management is the most difficult workforce engagement task for businesses today. More than 60 percent of businesses don't find it easy to identify and nurture future management.

- Companies that use online methods for building company culture are 38 percent more satisfied with their employee engagement than are those who don't interact with their employees online. More than three-quarters of the companies that use online methods to build company culture think they do a good job engaging hourly employees.

What's more, Ryan says, "If you ask anyone, from a third-shift guy to a part-time person, what his reason is for being a Roadrunner, he can tell you our mission statement," which is "to delight the customer in a way that makes them come back tomorrow. Roadrunner Markets will be the best convenience store retailer in the eyes of our customers, competitors and our employees." It's a great example of how focusing on culture and engaging employees has made a real, noticeable difference.

## Action Items

- Make sure you have a system in place to provide effective feedback to your employees, whether they are paid hourly or are salaried.
- Find ways to publically appreciate employees for good performance, such as the shout-outs we do at PeopleMatter during our weekly patio meetings. The effort holds so much meaning and power and costs nothing for the company to do.
- Look for ways to make personal connections with employees, whether through technology or in-person events.

# CHAPTER 6

# Drive the Downstream Impact

**ALL THE STUFF I HAVE TALKED** about in the previous three chapters—thinking about people in a new way, getting the right people in your company through better hiring practices, engaging them in new ways through the use of technology and inspiring them to grow and aspire higher—have a kind of ripple effect or what I call a downstream impact on the business. If we get all these things right up front, then, downstream, you are going to see the benefits. You get the lag measures, which are really the things you can see, such as increased sales, lower turnover, and higher customer satisfaction ratings, because the customers really enjoyed interacting with the employees they came into contact with in your stores. These are the kind of outcomes you can expect from all the investments and changes you have made upstream. This is really your return on your investment (ROI) in people.

Now, there's the tangible ROI and then there's also the intangible ROI. The tangible ROI is going to be those hard, objective measurements that I just talked about. But I also think there are subjective returns on your investment to consider. That cashier in Georgia, the single, hard-working mom I mentioned earlier, is an example of these subjective returns. The investments her company made in her through training and engagement and through showing her that she and her contribution were valued helped her feel better about herself. She felt more valued and inspired by knowing she was able to help the organization out. She felt she had a future there and a shot at a real career rather than continuing to struggle to make ends meet for herself and her kids. All that was going to bleed into her personal life, because if she was happier in her workplace, she was probably going to be happier at home too. Being able to make that sort of impact on someone's life is a really motivating and inspiring thing. That's a return on investment that I think employers and managers should consider, as well.

Because of all those positives, that cashier will have a beneficial long-term impact on the business. She is likely to stay longer because she sees a future there, which reduces the company's turnover rates. She will have more positive interactions with customers because she's happier and better trained, which will lead to repeat business, higher sales, and positive word-of-mouth marketing. There will be higher standards in the workplace because she takes pride in what she does, which affects her coworkers and customers alike. The two things— the tangible and intangible ROIs—affect each other. What's good for her is also good for the business.

Rewind to the beginning of this book when we talked about PeopleMatter's purpose and how we are a purpose-driven company. The purpose that we ground ourselves on is to change the way the employer and employee interact in the workplace and to make it better. There are tangible and intangible benefits from that purpose that we see every day, and those are the reasons why we do what we do each and every day.

For me, it's amazing to be able to walk into one of the stores that uses our PeopleMatter products and see a difference in the quality, demeanor and engagement of the people working there. We have been able to help people apply for and get jobs that they are a good fit for and we have been able to help organizations really take our brands to the next level by using their human capital to drive business outcomes and to differentiate themselves in the marketplace. Seeing the sort of difference we can make in people's lives is one of the most satisfying aspects of my career.

## Want To versus Have To

In the introduction to this book I talked about the formula I came up with when I first started to inspire innovation throughout PeopleMatter. It was Stimulate + Create = Innovate. That was my personal way of driving the downstream impact in my own company.

I began by hiring great people and providing them with an environment that is very stimulating in terms of the people they work with, the culture of the organization, and the physical environment in which they work. The first two—people and culture—are obvious parts of building a stimulating work environment, but I'm also a big believer in the value of place, the physical place where people work. A lot of companies today and a lot of the business books that are currently out there focus on things such as how to build a great culture and how to hire the right people, but I think not enough attention is paid to the physical space in which people work. I read an article that talked about how even the manner in which you organize team members—literally, who sits next to whom—has a huge impact on the ability of the business to be successful. That means that even employees' physical location within the business, down to where their desk is positioned, has an impact on how employees do their job. By putting different people next to each other, you can unlock interesting dynamics and discussions. It also makes people feel valued when they have a nice place to work. You don't have to have a fancy office, but clean restrooms, a nice kitchen area and things like that mean a lot to people.

Charleston Mayor, Joe Riley (center), held the ribbon-cutting honors at the 2013 grand opening of our 466 King Street headquarters. Every detail in the new building was planned with our Stimulate + Create = Innovate equation in mind.

When we designed our building for PeopleMatter, we looked at all sorts of things that could impact our team members in terms of not just their ability to do their work but also their enjoyment level at work. We paid particular attention to things such as color selection, different types of lighting, even what kind of desk would encourage collaboration. We looked at traffic flow (the physical movements of our team members within the workspace), which is a big consideration for service industry businesses as well, in terms of their customers' traffic movements. Restaurants, convenience stores, and similar retailers are always thinking about how to move consumers through their premises. They're asking things such as "How do we get them inside?" and once inside, "How do we get them to see more of the product?" Grocery stores put the milk in the back of the store, for example, because it's something people buy regularly and stores want to encourage customers to walk through the store to get it. In the process, they pass by a bunch of other products that might capture their attention.

We had similar things in mind when we did the layout for our office space. We looked closely at ways to encourage the kind of traffic flow we wanted. For instance, we have our demo rooms that our salespeople use up on the third floor where the engineers are, because, otherwise, the salespeople would never venture up to see the engineers and hang out with them. Similarly, we have the kitchen on the second floor where the salespeople are, so the engineers will venture down there and create interactions. We also have a really nice rooftop patio for people to gather on and socialize. In all these ways and more, we encourage collaboration and conversation, which leads to friendships and helps us build a stronger company.

The lesson here isn't that you have to design an office space like ours. The lesson is that we made all these decisions, down to the finest details of what kind of lighting we were going to use, with our team members in mind. Businesses are used to designing environments with the customer in mind, especially in the service industry. But I believe you have to take the employee into account too. When we designed our office space, of course we were thinking about clients coming to the office and the sort of impression we'd make. But we also thought about how this decision or that one was going to affect our people and whether there was a better way of doing something that would make for a more collaborative, more stimulating working environment.

Getting back to my formula for innovation, the environment we created makes up the *Stimulate* part of the equation. Then, if you stimulate your team members in the right way, they will bring the next part of the equation, which is the *Create* part. The employees will bring their creativity and passion to the work they do. They will really put their fingerprints on the business and on the products that are offered. And that is how we get *Innovation.*

The idea behind all this is to inspire people so they *want to* come to work rather than *have to* come to work every day. The trend of gamification in the workplace, which we talked about earlier, is all about this. Make something more fun—a training module or a business process—and people will *want* to engage in it rather than *feeling obliged* to engage in it. That is a really different mindset for people to have, and one that can lead to much better results.

User experience is what separates software that works from software that's going to change your life. Our product teams understand intuitive design like no one else and are masters at making powerful technology incredibly simple.

We have the same concept in mind when we build our software. We want it to be easy to use and fun, and we want it to look great. Software should be enjoyable to use! Every decision about the UI, or user interface (i.e., the colors, the look, the feel of the page, whether you're on a mobile device or a desktop computer), and about the UX, or user experience (i.e., how you actually move through the product and the flow of information) is made with people in mind. We are always asking ourselves how our software will inspire the users of our product. The feedback we consistently get is that people really appreciate our technology for its simplicity, because it's crisp and clear, because it makes what they have to do easier. It also appeals to a wide audience of diverse backgrounds.

Even something as simple as the hiring experience—the look and feel of the software companies used for application and onboarding processes—can set the tone for what a person's future experience is going to be like as an employee. It's either going to turn people on or turn them off. They are either going to say this looks like a fun, cool, hip company to work for or it looks like it's going to be a royal pain to work for. That's another example of a downstream effect right there: the first impression you make when you bring someone into your company can affect your relationship with that employee for years to come. The downstream impact of an easy and effective hiring process is that you get better-quality candidates who want to come work for you. Our customers have told us often that this is what happens when they start using our platforms for hiring and onboarding new employees.

## Tool: Stimulate + Create = Innovate

You can use this formula to drive the downstream impact in your business. The first part is *Stimulate*, by which I mean that it's the company's job to provide its people with a culture and environment that stimulates them to work hard for their organization. If the management team does that well, then the employees will bring the *Create* piece, because they will be passionate about what they do and about doing it well. The sum of these two parts is *Innovate,* which is how any company stays ahead of its competitors. It's how a company continues to grow and dominate its marketplace. Think about what you can do to provide your people with a stimulating workplace today, which will drive innovation—the downstream impact—tomorrow.

## The Downstream Impact

This chapter is about those outcomes you can expect to see if you put into practice many of the ideas in this book. The following case studies and customer stories highlight the return on investment that some of the companies we work with have seen by making investments in their people and in our products. These are companies that really aspire to help their people beyond just solving a business problem. They make investments in their culture, and they are among the top-tier performers in their respective categories as a result. And they've become some of the best performers in their categories. A PeopleMatter customer has won *Convenience Store Decisions'* Chain of the Year award for the past four years, from the year we were founded in 2009 through this past year. And I know our customers are going to continue sweeping these types of awards, because they look at not just the efficiency that comes from automating a process but also at how they're going to create a cultural shift through the use of our technology. We are lucky to be one piece of that big equation.

I can tell you more about all the great things that you can do in your business by starting with the simple idea that people matter, but I'd rather end by showing you what the outcomes can be if you do all these things. These are examples of what I call the downstream impact.

## Customer Story: Fastrac Markets

Fastrac is a convenience store operation in central New York. Dave Hogan is its Vice President of Human Resources and his focus is on reducing turnover. He has used PeopleMatter to help ensure that his hiring managers are spending enough time going through the candidate pool to find qualified candidates. One of the ways in which we were able to help him was by building a custom report that he could use to track how his hiring managers were doing. He could then set and track goals for them on the number of candidates they were interviewing and help them to understand how to use the assessment results to make better hiring decisions and increase their efficiency.

Fastrac saw a "marked improvement" in turnover, most notably due to the impact assessments have had on increasing applicant quality in each store. Dave said assessments have also increased hiring managers' productivity by allowing them to spend their time "interviewing those who truly are the *best* potential candidates to hire." As a result, Fastrac stores have been able to continually meet and exceed its hiring goals, and that directly affects the brand's bottom line.

## Customer Story: Family Express

Family Express is a smaller chain of convenience stores that has a heavy focus on hiring the right profile. The company looks to hire people whose personalities are inclined toward building relationships. The management team considers the workforce to be a competitive advantage, calling it "the living brand." Family Express team members are even authorized to send flowers to a customer if that's useful in maintaining or preserving the relationship. Family Express was one of our first custom benchmarking clients and was passionate about leveraging the culture it had built and getting that codified into a custom assessment that could be used for hiring processes. The company was so committed to ensuring the long-term success of its hiring processes that it signed a 15-year contract with us. That's the longest one we've signed so far.

...................................

## CASE STUDY: DOUBLEBEE'S CONVENIENCE STORES

Headquartered in Sercy, Arkansas, Doublebee's operates 28 convenience stores and started using PeopleMatter products in 2012. After hiring nearly 200 employees through the PeopleMatter Platform, the company determined the following:

- The company terminated 91 fewer employees in the fourth quarter of 2012 than it had in same quarter the previous year.

- Its turnover rate after using PeopleMatter went from 107.21 percent to 63.46 percent—a reduction of 43.75 percent.

- Not having to train 91 new employees saved the company well over $20,000 in training hours alone.

- Cash shortages in 28 locations were reduced by $10,000.

- Inventory shrinkage was .67 percent of sales for the year. (The industry standard is .75 percent.)

- The company has seen marked improvements in those hard-to-quantify but nonetheless important elements of the business, such as customer service, clean restrooms and the overall appearance of stores.

## CASE STUDY: NOODLES & COMPANY

Noodles & Company is a fast-casual restaurant concept that offers the world's favorite noodle dishes, sandwiches, salads and soups, all in one restaurant. Before partnering with PeopleMatter, the company needed to streamline its workforce management processes. It was using multiple, disparate point solutions across its more than 275 locations, which could not communicate with each other or work together as a whole.

PeopleMatter eliminated the disparate software systems and offered one, integrated, easy-to-use platform for workforce management processes. This streamlined the work, decreased the risk of noncompliance, as well as payroll and data-entry errors, and saved money in annual software upgrades.

**Return on Investment**
- Through better integration, time-to-hire was reduced by 99 percent.

- Managers had more time to focus on developing their team members and increasing guest satisfaction.

**Customer Reaction**
"PeopleMatter gave our restaurants a powerful, yet simple, system to manage time-consuming hiring and onboarding processes."
**–Alison Meadows, VP, Human Resources**

## FINDINGS FROM PMI'S *HOW HOURLY WORKFORCES WORK* SURVEY

Managers using multiple hiring systems are 2.5 times more likely to spend 10+ hours a week on hiring-related tasks, compared to those using a workforce management system.

# CASE STUDY: SCOTTY'S BREWHOUSE

Scotty's Brewhouse is a local chain of neighborhood pubs headquartered in Indianapolis, Indiana. The company has been growing very quickly, and as it expanded from five to nine locations, it discovered that its manual hiring process was holding it back. The time-consuming, paper-based process that was in place had a negative impact on both productivity and customer satisfaction. Restaurant managers were struggling to keep locations fully staffed, to keep track of all their applicants, and to maintain the required paperwork.

PeopleMatter helped the company streamline the hiring process by integrating applicant tracking, screening, I-9, and onboarding tools so the company could manage the entire process for all locations on one platform. The company also used our pre-screening and filtering features for hiring, which helped it identify dependable, service-minded job candidates more quickly. The impact has been a savings in both time and money as well as better-quality hires. As the company's director of HR put it, "PeopleMatter allows us to identify candidates who believe in what they are doing and strive to be great."

**Return on Investment**

- The company decreased time-to-hire by 77 percent, or 23 days.

- It saw an annual onboarding savings of $124,800.

- It increased hiring and I-9 compliance to 100 percent.

- It increased returns from tax credits by approximately 115 percent.

- It significantly reduced the number of interviews conducted each week.

- It decreased time spent completing hiring tasks by 5–10 hours per location each week.

**Customer Reaction**

"We are all looking at the black-and-white numbers, but we're still in the business of relationships. The great thing about working with PeopleMatter is the PeopleMatter team. I know that what I'm doing is not only affecting my bank statement and giving me positive results—helping my turnover, reducing expenses, helping the culture of my company—but also, at the end of the day, I know PeopleMatter is right there to help me build relationships."

**—Scott Wise, Founder and CEO**

## CASE STUDY: FLASH FOODS

Flash Foods is a convenience store chain headquartered in Waycross, Georgia, with close to 200 locations. When its paper-based human resources processes didn't make the cut, the company began searching for a solution that could save it time and money through automated hiring. At the same time, it was looking to update its training procedures. With a reputation for friendly service, Flash Foods needed a system that could quickly and easily identify, onboard and train a large volume of service-minded employees.

PeopleMatter provided Flash Foods with integrated hiring and training tools to help it manage human resources processes with more consistency and efficiency.

**Return on Investment**
- The company saved 3,980 hours of hiring managers' time.

- It reduced turnover by 40 percent.

- It increased tax-credit submissions by more than 195 percent in the first three months.

- Employees completed required training four months ahead of schedule.

- Training completion improved 73 percent and became 100 percent consistent.

**Customer Reaction**
"Ensuring your team is fully trained is the best way to save on existing labor—and that's what PeopleMatter LEARN™ is helping us do."
**—Jenny Bullard, Chief Information Officer**

...................................

## CASE STUDY: MAD GREENS– INSPIRED EATS

MAD Greens is a Colorado-based restaurant chain dedicated to helping people eat better by providing healthy foods that are made fresh with locally sourced ingredients. However, its paper-based hiring process needed a fresher approach. Human resources staff and restaurant managers were struggling to sort through hundreds of applications; to complete the necessary paperwork in a timely and accurate manner; and to track all requirements, deadlines and updates.

PeopleMatter provided MAD Greens with a comprehensive platform to integrate applicant tracking, screening and onboarding. This allowed the company to improve the efficiency and consistency of its operations, and to streamline its hiring and onboarding processes.

### Return on Investment
- The company decreased the time managers spent on hiring by 50 percent and time-to-hire by 11 days.

- It increased employee-record accuracy by 80 percent.

- It ensured 100-percent compliance with automated workflows.

- It improved candidate quality with pre-hire assessments.

### Customer Reaction
"Hiring people before PeopleMatter was hit or miss. It wasn't as organized and it was tough to monitor the efficiency and quality of the hiring we were doing."
**—Marley Hodgson, President and CEO**

......................................

# CASE STUDY: BOLOCO

Boloco is a local restaurant chain that is based in Boston, Massachusetts, and serves "globally inspired burritos." It is dedicated to its mission "to positively impact the lives and futures of our people through bold and inspired food and practices." The company was actually one of PeopleMatter's first customers. The Boloco team discovered us because they were Googling the term *people matter.* Cofounder John Pepper and his team had included a section on the company's website called "People Matter," where they talked about the people-focused values of their company. But as Pepper says, "A people-focused philosophy doesn't work on its own. It may distinguish us from competitors, but if you don't couple that with best-in-class operations, if you don't understand where to be disciplined, then it doesn't work." The company came to us for help in making some of its processes work more efficiently and effectively.

Before PeopleMatter, the company conducted all workforce management processes manually. Hiring practices were disconnected and took considerable amounts of time. Costly training investments were too often lost in turnover, due to new hires who were not committed to their positions. PeopleMatter provided the growing company with a customized online job application and survey and a comprehensive platform to connect and streamline its workforce management processes. This allowed it to identify dedicated candidates, and to hire and onboard them quickly.

**Return on Investment**
- The company improved productivity by 25 percent.

- It reduced turnover by 35 percent.

- It showed an 849 percent return on investment in just two months.

- It saw an annual benefit of $296,010.

**Customer Reaction**
"PeopleMatter's tools provide a simple, engaging way to connect our teams, culture and brand."
**–John Pepper, Cofounder and former CEO**

....................................

# CASE STUDY: SOUPER SALAD

Souper Salad is a chain of "all-you-care-to-eat" soup and salad bar restaurants located across the southern and western United States. Prior to consulting PeopleMatter, the company used mostly a paper-based hiring process that was inconsistent and time consuming. It was also not taking advantage of Work Opportunity Tax Credits or other hiring incentives.

PeopleMatter's integrated applicant tracking, onboarding, I-9 and tax credit tools automated the company's hiring processes, enabling it to increase compliance, reduce turnover, save time and improve data consistency.

**Return on Investment**
- The company saw a 40 percent increase in the number of employees qualifying for tax credits.

- It reduced time spent on new-hire paperwork by 94 percent.

- It saved $124,000 in mangers' time, which breaks down as $25,000 per year in assistant general managers' time; $88,000 per year in general managers' time; and $11,000 per year in district managers' time.

- It condensed new-hire training into three days.

- It saw a 17 percent reduction in turnover.

**Customer Reaction**
"Right from the start, PeopleMatter impressed us with their awesome products and their efficient, professional manner. This approach inspired confidence and produced the results we needed."
**–Souper Salad Director of Human Resources**

...............................

# CASE STUDY: THE PALM RESTAURANT GROUP

The first Palm restaurant opened in New York City in 1926. Today the Washington, DC-based restaurant group operates 25 fine-dining locations across the United States and in Mexico. Before working with PeopleMatter, the company's paper-based hiring process was time consuming and "frustrating," according to Director of HR Marc Hinson.

PeopleMatter helped the group streamline its hiring processes and automate its application, I-9, and onboarding forms; this has saved the company time and effort and helped get better quality hires on board more quickly. By utilizing PeopleMatter SCHEDULE™, the restaurant group is also able to provide its team members with online tools and a free mobile app that helps improve employee communication and scheduling efficiency.

**Return on Investment**
- The company quadrupled its application volume, while decreasing its time-to-hire.

- It saved 438 hours annually, from onboarding alone.

- It saved, on average, $1,139 per month on onboarding labor costs.

- Managers saved, on average, 30 minutes per hire, when processing I-9s.

- The company saved, on average, $1,139 each month on onboarding labor costs.

**Customer Reaction**
"My favorite thing is PeopleMatter's ability to filter and screen applicants. All of the information is there. I don't have to back out to send an e-mail or forward a résumé. I totally dig the 'one stop shop' aspect."
**–Marc Hinson, Director of HR**

# FINDINGS FROM PMI'S *HOW HOURLY WORKFORCES WORK* SURVEY

- Companies that use online methods for building company culture are 38 percent more satisfied with their employee engagement than those who don't interact with their employees online.

- More than three-quarters of companies that use online methods to build company culture think they do a good job of engaging hourly employees.

# More Than Lip Service

**BY THIS POINT,** I hope I have shown just how vitally important it is to your business that you really understand that your people matter. But this is about more than just knowing that people matter; you have to know how to show it too. It can't just be a slogan on your wall or a policy in your manual. It has to be something that you work on and demonstrate on a daily basis.

To demonstrate that our people matter to me, I really want to brag about my team here. Our PeopleMatter team members are some of the most awesome people I have ever had the pleasure to work with. Beyond that, we have built meaningful friendships and relationships within the workplace, and they truly motivate me to aspire higher each and every day, to push PeopleMatter to be a better company, to push PeopleMatter to be a bigger company, to push PeopleMatter to constantly challenge the status quo, and to push myself to live up to these high aspirations.

I want to thank the entire team for all the hard work it does to serve our customers. The customer service team that deals with the questions and inquiries from users about our products; the engineering and product team members who build our products and dream up all the features that go into them and the plans for future products. All of these people play a tremendous role in the success we have had so far in the business, and their dedication and creativity will allow us to continue to be an extremely successful company.

It has been an awesome experience working with such a talented group of folks. It's the thing that gets me up each morning. We are on a journey to build a large company, and I mean large in the sense of the impact that we will have on millions of lives—everybody from that single working mom with two kids from Georgia, to the individuals starting their own businesses, to the shareholders of some of our bigger customers. Those are the people I want us to have a positive impact on. That's where I believe we can pay more than lip service to these ideas and the overall theme that people matter. We walk the walk every day, and we are really challenging ourselves to constantly be better at what we do.

There are also some individual teams and team members that I would like to single out here, so I can express my appreciation to them for all that they do. Every one of these people either works directly for me or has been with us for a long period of time, and they all have had a tremendous impact on the success of the business.

I would like to thank **Ken Haigh**, Chief Operating Officer. He is the guy who really keeps our operation humming along in such an incredible way. He is one of the smartest human beings I have ever worked with in my career. Just tremendously intelligent and thoughtful, he adds the keel on the ship with his stability to the team.

I would like to thank **Nancy Sansom**, Senior Vice President of Marketing and Human Resources. She is somebody whom I have had the pleasure of working with for more than 10 years at two different companies—Benefitfocus and now PeopleMatter. I consider her to be a sister. We move in unison in what we do. We know how to read each other. We know how to challenge each other. She is somebody who is always coming up with creative ways to get our message and our brand out there into the marketplace.

I would like to thank **Michael Wright,** Vice President of Technology. I am continually amazed at his leadership and perseverance. He keeps the momentum rolling day in and day out for our engineering teams, and I have never seen someone gain as much respect from their team as Michael. He is just an amazing human being who brings a wealth of perspective and value to the organization.

I would like to thank **Kenny Oubre,** Senior Director of Customer Success, who has been instrumental in getting our sales and implementation engines running. He's been at PeopleMatter from nearly day one and is a huge reason we are as successful as we are today. I am extremely thankful for all that he has done for the company; his unwavering support of me has been tremendously impactful to my success, both personally and professionally.

I would like to thank **Jay Bredenberg,** one of the most talented and gifted software architects that I have ever met. Jay is one of those rare people who is both incredibly brilliant and incredibly down-to-earth. He is a tremendous asset for the company and for our engineering team.

I would like to thank **Kay Lucas,** Vice President of Product Management. She works tirelessly to keep our products on the cutting edge and exemplifies the essence of hard work, dedication, and commitment. She always takes the time to talk to our customers and potential customers and to really understand what they want. I am very thankful for the passion and drive that she brings to our products and to our company.

I would like to recognize our **customer experience team.** These are the individuals who deal with the day-to-day calls and support. I have often said that the success of our company will be determined by the experience that an applicant has on a Tuesday at 10:52 a.m.

When that applicant hangs up that phone, what feeling does he or she have after that call? Is it a great feeling of being valued and appreciated and having questions answered or problems solved? Or is it a not-so-great feeling? That difference will be the determination of our success, because that is what spreads goodwill toward PeopleMatter out into the marketplace.

I would also like to thank the spouses and partners of all the team members in our company and in all the companies we do business with. You are our unsung heroes. You are the ones who are oftentimes forgotten and overlooked because we don't see you day in and day out. But you are the ones who support the team members every day and allow them to go to their jobs and work hard to make a difference. Whether you are the spouse or partner of a convenience store clerk, a retail clerk, a manager of a restaurant, or one of our own team members, I never lose sight of you and the contribution you make to our success.

........................................

Making changes to your business to ensure that your people really matter takes attention and persistence, but it doesn't have to be all that hard to do. As with anything in business, you need the right perspective, the right tools, a plan and some discipline to get it done. It's really about consistent focus and discipline. But I believe the payoff can be about more than just saving time or cutting costs. Those things are certainly important, but there is a bigger value that comes from appreciating people, investing in people and using technology as a catalyst for those things. It's about making sure that every person in your business has a real meaning and a real purpose out there in the world. Your people are the most valuable and important piece of your company. They are the ones who will help you solve your business problems every day. They are the ones who will help you grow your top line and your bottom line. You couldn't accomplish any of your business goals without them, and they should really feel valued because of that.

At PeopleMatter, this is the kind of change that we plan to facilitate. We are aiming to be the largest global provider of workforce management products and services for the service industry. We are in this for the long haul. We are grounded by our purpose, and we know that if we stay grounded by our purpose, then all the financial benefits will come. We always want to aspire higher and find new ways to bring more value to the employer-employee relationship. We truly are on a mission to serve millions of people, and we believe there is a wealth of opportunity out there for change.

That is what we are committed to doing. My hope is that this book will inspire some folks to make similar commitments of their own, to take that next step and start to implement a change for the better in their organizations.

Printed in the USA
CPSIA information can be obtained
at www.ICGtesting.com
JSHW050802160824
68134JS00071B/121/J